The Breeze of the Spirit

The Breeze of the Spirit

Sam Shoemaker and
the Story of Faith at Work

IRVING HARRIS

A *Crossroad Book* / The Seabury Press / *New York*

To my teammates the kindred spirits
whose faith and experience
created this book

1978 / The Seabury Press
815 Second Avenue / New York, N.Y. 10017

Library of Congress Cataloging in Publication Data
Harris, Irving D   The breeze of the spirit.
"A Crossroad book."
1. Shoemaker, Samuel Moor, 1893–1963.   2. Protestant
Episcopal Church in the U.S.A.—Clergy—Biography.
3. Clergy—United States—Biography.   4. Faith at
work. I. Title.
BX5995.S347H37   283'.092'4 [B]   78-18237
ISBN 0-8164-0399-6

High Flight*
Lt. John Gillespie Magee, Jr.

Oh, I have slipped the surly bonds of earth
    And danced the skies on laughter-silvered wings,
Sunward I've climbed and joined the tumbling mirth
    Of sun-split clouds—and done a hundred things
You have not dreamed of—wheeled and soared and swung
    High in the sunlit silence. Hov'ring there
I've chased the shouting wind along and flung
    My eager craft through footless halls of air.
Up, up the long delirious, burning blue
    I've topped the windswept heights with easy grace
Where never lark, or even eagle flew.
    And, while with silent, lifting mind I've trod
The high untrespassed sanctity of space,
    Put out my hand, and touched the face of God.

—from *The Calvary Evangel* of May, 1942,
and the 1942 paperback *What It Takes*

* This sonnet was written by an American pilot in the RCAF who lost his life over England at the age of nineteen. It is a classic expression of courage combined with faith. The original manuscript was exhibited in the Library of Congress with poems by Burns, Shelley, Longfellow, Joyce Kilmer, and others.

Contents

Author's Preface

*I*t was a brand new time. It was a bright and shining time, this much anticipated new age. At first the horizon of the twentieth century flamed with orange and gold. The very atmosphere was invigorating. As a schoolboy I felt quite sure it was a good time to be alive.

The inventors had done their job. Main Street blazed with electric lights, and before long black wires were seen stretching from house to house. Boy, you could talk over them! And the voices were real and could be understood. The day we got our 'phone smacked of Christmas: "708—party M."

Business flourished. The State of New Jersey displayed the words "Progress" and "Prosperity" on its shield as an established fact. Britannia ruled the waves. With the Spanish-American War over, it was widely assumed that peace was established forever. For over fourteen years America enjoyed the experience of freewheeling and expansion.

Then, unexpectedly, the colors faded and in Europe turned pitch-black. Even so, the fields of Flanders seemed very far away and a respite ensued under a president who, for awhile, kept us out of war. A senseless war, 'twas said, between nations declared Christian.

In the end, the vast majority of us were caught up in the fighting. For a few, enlistment led to unbelievable horror; but most American students managed to stay on the fringe of the world crisis where they flirted with danger but usually suffered only trifling upsets, often no worse than the humiliation I had one morning in Stern's Department Store when an affable shopper mistook my brand-new Navy blue uniform and confidently addressed me as the elevator starter.

When the War suddenly ceased, the lucky enlistees like me tripped quietly back to dormitory and classroom, taking these privileges more seriously perhaps, but in countless instances, wondering who we were and what to expect next. The nation, for all its debates, remained firmly isolationist. Jazz and irresponsibility multiplied throughout the Northeast—for among the majority of our generation, who could care less? But the choice of a vocation, *any* vocation, became paramount.

These were the days when university graduates with decent marks had almost unlimited job openings, most of which seemed quite pleasant if not especially profitable. After one false start, happily and quite naïvely, I "favored" the old All-America Cables, Inc. Though completely untutored, I was pleased but not surprised to be made one of the assistants to the president. My shallow goals had simplified greatly and, frankly, had dwindled to two: a wife who, above all else, could dance, and a niche where we could feel "economically independent."

The cable company offered communication facilities between the Americas. When I discovered that the president had never visited a single overseas office, I became an ardent advocate of travel, with the result that I was given the responsibility of conducting the company's first family on a luxury tour of our cable stations in Brazil, Uruguay, and Argentina. My personal life-style continued to be "high, wide, and handsome."

From such high-flown materialism, however, I was most unexpectedly *and fortunately* rescued by a painful personal disaster more crippling than any event during my year in the Navy—an onslaught of undulant fever. At that time little was known about this disease beyond the fact that it had its origin in unpasteurized milk. As our party sailed homeward, a strange malaise took possession of me, a feeling of inertia punctuated by recurring periods of low fever. Presently, I had to resign my job in order to search for an antidote to my mysterious illness.

In turn, I tried medications, rest, psychology, and, during times of improvement, a change of occupation. Self-pity and negative thought patterns had a field day. No place or activity seemed tolerable for long.

Then a bright hope suddenly glimmered in the gloom, perhaps an inspired one if measured by subsequent events. The gleam focused on the halcyon summer days which I had enjoyed at Camp Dudley on the shore of Lake Champlain. In that most ancient of boys' summer camps there had repeatedly been offered me a chance for both physical growth and enriching friendship. I hastily wrote to ask what chance there might be to spend a few weeks at camp without undertaking the full responsibilities of a counselor.

Chief Beckman, the director, welcomed me back on a most unusual basis. I was simply to be the camp's guest, without any definite duties. Thus I settled in, swam a bit, and lazed my afternoons away in a canoe. I occasionally told a camp-fire story and took vespers in a tent whose leader was absent.

A series of Sunday morning religious services were an important feature of the camp's spiritual program. Here, weather permitting, some three hundred campers and leaders gathered in the shade of a wooded slope overlooking the lake to worship and to listen to a special speaker invited for the occasion.

One hot August morning the camp director found me writing letters on the counter in the camp store.

"Oh, there you are," he said rather abruptly. "I've come to tell you that you're preaching on Sunday."

Scarcely heeding, I made some facetious reply; but looking up I saw him peering at a Western Union telegram from one of our special speakers, an old-time favorite who had wired his cancellation because of ill health. "You see our friend can't come. I want you to give the boys a talk in his place."

Startled, I tried to explain that preaching was the last thing in the world that I could tackle—besides I was supposed to be ill.

"I think you can take care of it," the chief said, smiling. "You'll be surprised, old kid, how much can happen between now and Sunday."

Shoving my unanswered letters into a box, I walked down toward the lake shore to get a whiff of fresh air and to think. Like a Dr. Jekyll, Camp Dudley, with its focus on helping the other fellow, had always countered the Mr. Hyde nature which so often took possession of me at college. My custom was to allow an unselfish "Dudley spirit" to evaporate during the winter; yet in some degree at least it continued with me as an aspect of a better self. Here by the lake a question caught my imagination: "Why not talk about the vision of life which camp so often gives those who come here?" I could use as a basis the Apostle Paul's great experience on the road to Damascus. That had been more dramatic, but in essence I believe it was similar.

Returning to the store and slipping a fresh sheet of paper into my portable, I began a paragraph comparing Paul's unforgettable experience to the spiritual potential of current camp life. As I contemplated what had happened so long ago in Syria, I was given a second point—a man's need to allow a God-given vision to bring him to a *decision* about the future course of his life. Sermons, as I then thought, must have three points. Now, surely, it would take plenty of courage to carry out the practical steps of a costly, self-denying choice in any respect similar to St. Paul's.

Vision, decision, courage—not a very complicated message but precise and practical. As I typed paragraph after paragraph, the sermon fairly flowed and illustrations from camp life came flooding in.

Next morning I spent several hours at a spot where I had once been introduced to the mysteries of American Indian lore. With my manuscript in hand I read the talk over aloud: "The major decisions of life must be made as a result of, and in line with, one's vision." As I spoke this sentence, a funny thing happened. I suddenly realized that I was *already* preaching and already had an interested congregation—none other than *myself*. Surely God must have a sense of humor!

In the intervening days before Sunday I returned frequently to the Indian Council Ring to repeat the talk to the pine trees. Like the lines in a Triangle Show, I was convinced that my first sermon must be learned word for word. "Vision. Decision. Courage." But then with the repetition of these three points a question repeatedly arose, "What about yourself? What about yourself?"

Saturday afternoon arrived—my last rehearsal—and at last I saw quite clearly that one couldn't look out at a crowd of young boys, and at a group of friends who knew and loved you, and talk about a decision like St. Paul's unless he had made such a decision himself. I realized that I couldn't give what I had written without being a hypocrite unless I first accepted personally the whole thesis of the talk. I had come to the crossroads, and I knew I had to choose personally which road I would take.

It was late—but perhaps still not too late. My heart gave a bound, and for a moment everything around me—the birds' songs, the wind in the pines, all the wood sounds—seemed to cease as though Someone were waiting expectantly. Finally, I looked up through the pines at the blue, blue sky. My lips opened and I said a few words and the words were ones of freedom and of joy; "O God, if You can still use me, at last I am ready to say yes."

There was a sudden indescribable lightness of body and mind. It was as if a load had fallen from my shoulders, and then, with great joy, I repeated the end of the talk over and over again.

And what a joy it proved the next day—a fresh and sunny morning with the air touched by a piney fragrance and the light upon the water glistening through the trees! I looked out at that special sea of faces, confident not so much of myself as of the worth and integrity of what I had to say.

A couple of days later I told a group of friends that (guess what?) I had decided to study for the ministry. As I expected, they were both amused and highly delighted.

*　　*　　*

As I began looking over catalogues from Virginia Theological Seminary and New College, Edinburgh, I kept thinking of the contract I had recently signed with the Princeton University Press to become their first advertising manager. In good conscience I could hardly sidestep this simply because I had changed my mind about my own vocation. The agreement called for being in Princeton by mid-August, so it was up to me to leave the Adirondacks almost immediately.

That summer "the best old place of all" was about the hottest old place of all, but my new job far exceeded expectations. Frequent excursions to the big city, where Scribner's, E. P. Dutton & Co., Putnam, and other publishers were located, brought me in touch with older advertising men who were more than happy to get personal service on any accounts with the *Princeton Alumni Weekly,* and I rarely returned empty-handed.

This agreeable schedule, however, was upset within a matter of weeks. The eminent editor of *The Weekly,* Edwin M. Norris, became seriously ill and was forced to take an immediate leave of absence.

"Ted" Norris knew the names of almost every living alumnus and had carried on a notable work at the Press for more than twenty years. But there was no help for it; a raw recruit must be transferred across the courtyard into the editorial sanctum and there see what he could do. Various kinds of manuscripts for the first issue of Volume XXV, dated October 1, 1924, were piling up and somehow it was up to me to cope with them. I didn't see how it could be done, but I'd certainly take a shot at it.

Everyone chipped in to get things off the ground. I was introduced to the boss of the pressroom, down the corridor, where I also shook hands with the linotype operator who set every word of copy for the magazine. The chief designer and the layout men were at my beck and call. The mysteries of different type faces became commonplace knowledge, and there was always Mr. Norris in a rocker on his side porch to correct me and cheer me on. I relished the work and my periodic fever nearly vanished.

Soon I renewed contact with Sam Shoemaker. As a former secretary of the campus religion foundation, he continued to visit Princeton and follow up his quest for more and better men for the ministry. And what a man he was with his glorious sense of humor and the appearance of a football player! As an undergraduate I had been his constant critic. I felt he wanted every one of us to become a clergyman, and perhaps he did. After the experience at camp, and a radical change of direction, I hoped to focus on God's concerns as much as he, but not necessarily within the exact Shoemaker context.

One Sunday afternoon, Sam asked me if I had seen a modern translation of the New Testament by a Scotsman, Professor James Moffatt. I hated such questions and shied away from this one. "My upbringing and church training," I thought to myself, "have made me plenty familiar with the Bible and, besides, I've got much more important things to study now."

But sooner or later most of Sam's suggestions bore fruit, so I ordered a copy of the Moffatt translation, and back in my room I secretly launched a new devotional program. I started with the book of Mark, as this was the shortest Gospel. To my intense surprise I reveled in the fresh language and the clearer picture of Christ which the pages revealed. In my imagination I saw Jesus traveling dusty roads, visiting villages, and entering Jerusalem. The whole story had a continuity which I had previously missed, and in the contacts and situations of his first-century days I could see counterparts in the campus life at Princeton.

Early one morning I took a yellow pad and listed a few of the chief characteristics of the amazing person I was coming to know: complete openness, humility plus courage, rare unselfishness, unfailing love. A few days later, I drew a line across the middle of the page and began to put down attitudes and events in my life which were the direct opposites of those listed above. All too vividly I remembered: exaggerations which often turned the truth into a false impression, tall stories retold to make a hit, profits of the senior prom committee on which I had made only a partial accounting.

The morning I found that my list totaled twenty-nine, I dropped down by the bedside as if I were a child; I felt rather like the Prodigal Son, overwhelmed by a sense deeper than remorse and truly wanting a chance to do better. Then it happened, an experience much deeper than the one at camp. I cried out for forgiveness and I suddenly knew that God was giving me just that. I felt humiliated and uplifted at the same moment with the slate washed clean and the inner freedom I needed. At breakfast downstairs the bacon and eggs tasted like ambrosia.

Camp Dudley had indicated the new direction I should take. Now I saw how to chart the course.

*　　*　　*

The chapters of this book overflow with stories. They are not so much the author's tales as personal reports of lives which, decade by decade, have overcome the turmoil of our times. The stories concern all kinds of men and women who have at least one thing in common: they share the same goals and have each made some of the same spiritual discoveries.

Many readers will remember Sam Shoemaker and the quality of living he and his friends describe. Others may be strangers to Faith at Work. The point is that everyone, with God's help, can attain victorious living, and as Bill Wilson used to say, *maintain* it. Surely a new world begins with new lives, and those who are born again give thanks, march on, and rejoice as they go.

Irving Harris
Princeton, New Jersey
November, 1978

1 /

A Shoemaker on Gramercy Park

A remarkable chain of events which revived a moribund Manhattan church, and subsequently touched the lives of men and women in a hundred countries 'round the world, began in mid-May, 1925, when a curly-haired young Southerner walked slowly through the dark and rather gloomy sanctuary of Calvary Church, New York. Only the polished pews and the lights of the altar brightened the interior of the old building. Sam Shoemaker, who had been visiting centers of Christian work abroad, may well have wondered if he had made a mistake in exchanging the sunny skies of India for anything as drab and unprepossessing as this dirt-colored edifice. But a few days later, as the Sunday service began, the new rector's natural buoyancy had returned. A good sized congregation contributed a general sense of expectancy, and he spoke his well-prepared words with a sure knowledge that they were true, appropriate, and timely.

"Our country is desperately weak," he said in part, "especially in having churches where men and women in search of a vital, firsthand experience of the living God may expect to find the clergy eagerly on the lookout for them, prepared to give them time and personal help, to listen to their stories, to take time for them one by one. . . ."

Halfway through, and by no means as a digression, the new preacher then spoke in a different vein: "I am no believer in a narrowly individualistic religion which will not let itself go out to grapple with those social and industrial and racial and international questions which affect us all in our corporate aspect."

As he returned to his main thrust, a personal one, he concluded, "I was told that this was a congregation which would like to have their church become a kind of spiritual powerhouse and minister to the needs of as many in this great city as should care to come to us. I am immensely drawn to the possibility of working in a church where with one mind and one heart we might set out to create a genuine center of spiritual energy."

Prophetic words? Later on many were to think so.

On the porch, following the service, the young clergyman was surrounded by enthusiastic admirers. The warm spring air fairly shimmered with promise. Actually this inaugural Sunday, with its influx of young men and women, was succeeded in years to come by over a thousand similar occasions. The content of the message would differ in certain respects as the years went by but the Spirit continued to flow with power from Calvary's pulpit, and Shoemaker's purpose ever remained the same—to bring counsel, caution, and clarity to men and women who, in America's changing scene, were seeking a richer, freer personal life.

Few who knew Sam Shoemaker could pinpoint with certainty the influences that brought this young son of the Green Spring Valley of Maryland to Gramercy Park, New York. Several factors clearly contributed, but in God's strange providence a tea party in Peking, China, proved crucial. It was wartime in 1918 when young Shoemaker, recently graduated from college, was serving on the faculty of a business school which Princeton University helped to maintain for Chinese boys who wished to learn the rudiments of English and business methods. It was lodged in the Peking Christian Association.

While never a thoroughgoing pacifist, Sam Shoemaker had entertained many grave questions about the war in which some of his classmates had already lost their lives. A high draft number gave him latitude for choice. He recalled at the time the statement of an English leader: "Foreign missions are the one indisputably Christian flag flying at this moment." And so he had gone, not to a training camp at a place like Plattsburgh, New York, or in Newport, Rhode Island, but to a more exotic spot with a campus still dedicated to the arts of peace.

Few men got along with other people more easily than young Shoemaker. He not only had what is tritely called "a winning personality," but he influenced most of those with whom he associated so that they in turn enjoyed a measurable increase in self-esteem. The younger Chinese lads in his classes delighted him, especially those in the Bible class he was asked to teach soon after his arrival.

He had no reason to be dissatisfied. Certainly he was not hankering to be on the high seas or in Flanders, and yet things were not working out quite the way he wished. His chief concern proved to be the boys in the Bible class. Those who gathered 'round the stove in his room twice a week were supposed to be enquirers into the Christian faith. At the first meeting there were about twenty, at the next fourteen, and at the third exactly seven! My methods, he thought, must be faulty. But of course the trouble went deeper. He simply did not have the power to transmit his Anglican brand of faith to his students.

Then one day he heard of a small band of fellow countrymen who were visiting Peking, men who apparently did know how to channel God's power into the lives of those who wanted to know Him better. Shoemaker first went to hear them talk and soon afterwards called to see the leader, Frank Buchman. Encouraged by the latter's warmth, he explained his predicament, describing his home and church life in Maryland and how these good influences had turned him toward the ministry. When he got to the Chinese picture, he dwelt on the high quality of the lads in the Bible class and made bold to suggest that if Buchman could but touch one or two of the leaders of this group, they might well affect the whole student body.

Here one is presented with a scene worth analyzing: two men who, in succeeding years, may have touched effectively for Christ as many individuals as any two clergymen in the first half of the twentieth century: the older man aggressive, self-confident, and extremely astute in seeing behind people's masks and diagnosing an evil or a field of failure which was blocking the flow of the spirit; the other, Shoemaker, more kindly, less precise in his diagnosis, but equally eager to see lives kindled spiritually, and desirous above all to bring younger men into the ministry.

Thus far Buchman had followed Shoemaker's story with flattering attention. The rapport seemed complete until suddenly the older man stretched up his arms, leaned back, and laughed. He gave no advice, but to Shoemaker's surprise he asked a very personal question. "Tell me," he said abruptly. "Why don't you get through to at least *one* of these fellows—yourself?"

The younger man was ready for almost anything but this. Heretofore, religious leaders had invariably patted him on the back and told him how fine it was that he was going into the ministry. Now Shoemaker didn't like to be thus unexpectedly put on the spot; his pride was hurt and, since the best defense is often an offense, he countered with a question of his own: "If you know the trouble, why not tell me what it is?"

"Might be sin," Buchman replied, and then he went on to describe how resentment in his own life had for over a year kept him from spiritual freedom and power.

To say that Shoemaker was nettled would be greatly to understate his reaction. He quickly made his excuses, broke off the conversation, and walked home alone across the city, determined to take no part in such "morbid introspection."

But he couldn't get the conversation out of his mind, especially Buchman's reference to sin. He recalled that someone had once explained this three-letter word as any barrier, great or small, between oneself and God or between oneself and other people. He could see plenty of barriers in his own life. Several were what might be called "reserved areas." One had to do with his service in China. He had come out to the Far East on a short-term basis. Was he willing to stay on indefinitely should God indicate the necessity? He asked himself this and similar questions.

More troubled in mind than ever, as he ate supper he continued to consider the future—his personal life, marriage, the kind of a ministry that God might be calling him to—and then again (perhaps with animosity) he thought of Frank Buchman. How long this all took one would hesitate to guess, but there came a moment (was it ten o'clock? eleven? midnight?) when, unable to sleep and strangely moved, he finally slipped to his knees and entered into a wholly fresh spiritual transaction. He now realized how greatly he needed forgiveness. It seemed to him that he heard someone saying, "You want to do My work but in your own way." As the sense of God's love enfolded him, he then and there agreed that he would serve Him anywhere indefinitely. "Take me and use me, dear Father," he may have said, "without any of the old reservations. And thank You for the light revealed to me by my brother. Bless him and his friends and use us all in Your service."

While his words can only be guessed at, Shoemaker's act of dedication can be described with reasonable accuracy, for he later wrote about it much as Luke did in describing what happened to the Apostle Paul on a certain journey to Damascus. He reported that he felt no special emotion, but a great sense of relief because unfinished business had at last been settled and God had had His way. With a sense of new freedom and release, he then dropped off to sleep.

It so happened that on the morrow, by previous arrangement, he was having tea with one of his young Chinese friends. But long before this, he returned to the Princeton-in-Peking Center and, as he hoped, again found Frank Buchman.

"Frank," he blurted out, "you were right. Without realizing it, I have been a pious fraud, pretending to serve God but actually keeping all the trump cards in my own hands. Now I've told the Lord how sorry I am; and I trust that you will forgive me for harboring ill will against you. This sprang up the moment you used that word *sin!*"

As was his habit, Frank again laughed and said how glad he was that God had had His way, and how freely he forgave Sam personally for any negative attitudes toward himself. "It has been truly said that God has no work for him who is not wholly His. Now what's the next step?" he added.

"Ah, that's the heck of it," replied the other. "I feel like a new man but I haven't the ghost of an idea about what to say to the boy with whom I'm having tea. This is one of the fellows whom I wish more than ever to reach. But what shall I tell him?"

Like a shot Buchman answered, "Tell him just what you've told me. Just be honest about yourself."

Shoemaker sighed with relief. Of course. He quickly realized that he could tell the Chinese boy what God had done in his own life the night before. Laughingly, he thanked Buchman, got himself a rickshaw, and went along to the East City, still hesitant to some degree but newly aware that God was with him. As he approached his destination, several of his uncertainties returned. He remembered the language barrier and for a moment he almost wished that he would not find the boy at home. Then he knocked on the door and the young man welcomed him, bowing.

At the table there were things to be discussed about the school, and certain little formalities to be performed, but after each had had his second cup of tea, Shoemaker plunged in. "What I've said in the Bible classes has all been true, but I've just realized that I've been a downright hypocrite personally. A Christian yields himself to God, not only what he possesses but what he hopes to become. He trusts Him with his whole future. But until last night I had never done that." As the Chinese listened in rapt attention, he told him the story of his encounter with Frank Buchman and of the results. "And so, in the end," he concluded, "I knelt down and asked God to forgive me and to take me to be completely His own."

A pause followed, a kind of living silence. Then the Chinese said softly, "Last night you had a fresh, new experience of God. I wish that could happen to me now."

At this the two men talked briefly of the honesty and purity and faith required of any individual who gives his total allegiance to God, and when the student expressed his readiness they prayed together. It was a holy moment and each man felt deeply moved and very grateful.

After this many things became different in the school in Peking, and in the Bible class first of all. At the end of the school year, with the war over, Shoemaker returned to America, but not because he especially wanted it that way. It was quite apparent to him and to many others that more and more perplexed undergraduates in the United States were looking for help, while the self-indulgent level of American campus life cried out for leaders who would challenge it. When Princeton University needed a vigorous new secretary for the campus religious foundation, the trustees persuaded Shoemaker to take the post for a year before continuing his studies for the ministry. It was a time when many students were ready to consider seriously vocations which required personal sacrifice, and not a few found deeper faith and fresh direction by talking privately with him.

Then Sam became a student at General Theological Seminary in New York where, during his second year, the perceptive rector of nearby Grace Church, Dr. Charles Lewis Slattery, appointed him to his staff as a part-time assistant. He was now able to live in Grace Church House, off lower Broadway, where his student contacts continued and individuals, as well as groups of college-age young people, frequently sought him out for counsel.

After ordination, with the warm approval of his own bishop, he left the country again and with three other young university graduates, two of them British, traveled with Frank Buchman on an extended trip through Europe and the Middle East. It was Buchman's intention to bring succor and spiritual refreshment to teachers and doctors, in schools and mission hospitals, much as he had been doing on his earlier visit to Peking. As they worked, the "team" was also exploring the meaning of Christian discipleship and learning the discipline this required.

By 1924, a good many Easteners had heard of Sam Shoemaker's unusual power as a speaker, his fondness for student work, and his effectiveness in personal counseling. So it was not surprising that Calvary's enterprising vestry, realizing that new steps were desperately needed to preserve their trust, became aware of his existence and gifts. Under the leadership of George C. Zabriskie, a wise and eminent lawyer, and Henry Parish, a dedicated businessman, the Calvary vestry had not merely informed themselves about Shoemaker, they had considered all the related facts, as they knew them, and voted unanimously to issue him an immediate and rather urgent call.

It devolved upon Mr. Zabriskie to make the contact and present the Calvary picture and the conditions of their offer. He did this in a short cable and a long, registered letter, both addressed to Shoemaker, Care of Thomas Cook and Son, Cairo, Egypt. Of the church's various difficulties, about which Mr. Zabriskie was quite frank, he mentioned a dwindling congregation as the most serious. "We should not wish you to come to us," he wrote, "supposing our condition to be better than it is, or easy. In the past ten years the parish has declined. . . . We report to the Diocesan Convention something over eleven hundred communicants. I doubt if you could find so many. . . . The services are not well attended. . . and there are not many parishioners who [now] live in the neighborhood. They live in the Bronx and other more or less distant parts of the city; some live on Long Island or in New Jersey. We have about $500,000 of endowments [and] the value of our real estate probably exceeds $1,000,000 . . . [but] we are not getting an adequate spiritual return for the capital invested, the income received, and the labor exerted. . . . The vestry agrees with the bishop that we need intensive spiritual cultivation."

Shoemaker's cabled reply consisted of but twenty-two words and expressed no enthusiasm for the New York post. The majority of his traveling companions, set on the contribution they hoped to make to the life of the next Christian communities on their itinerary, viewed the call to Calvary Church as a genuine red herring. The gist of Shoemaker's cable read: JUDGMENT UNFAVORABLE NOW and the message ended: SAILING INDIA TODAY . . . WRITING.

But God had other plans. The team of four or five spent Christmas of 1924 in Madras, and Shoemaker, still uncertain, borrowed the home of some friends who were going out of town, and went there alone for two days. "I read the Bible and Fitchett's *Wesley and His Century*, and prayed," he reports. "I took a sheet of paper and put down on one side the reasons for accepting, and on the other side the reasons against it. . . . One formulates reasons . . . but one cannot quite reason out a growing conviction that one must take this direction or that, or the intensification of such a conviction in prayer. I came away from those two days of retreat, clear in my own mind that I should accept the call to Calvary Church."

And this he forthwith did.

2 /

The Old Rectory Explodes

When the vestry had been considering ways of solving the problem of Calvary Church's dwindling congregation, prior to extending a call to any successor to Dr. Sedgewick, several plans had been proposed. Many parishioners wished to move the congregation to a wholly new location, but this possibility was discarded when a few leading vestrymen gained support for their suggestion. They believed that the right man, a young clergyman with an imaginative program, could not only salvage but even greatly extend God's work on the very spot where it had already been carried on for almost a hundred years.

Because Sam Shoemaker believed this himself, Fourth Avenue and Twenty-first Street soon became hallowed ground for him and his friends. People from far and near also began to come to hear him preach and to attend meetings in the old brownstone rectory which adjoined the church.

Sam was a man to be reckoned with. Especially since his "encounter in Peking," his natural love for people crystallized into a keen desire to see them change from indolence and purely self-centered interests to the fuller, more purposeful life which he himself had found. He considered "the up and outs" as needy as "the down and outs."

A. J. Russell, a British journalist, in his best seller, *For Sinners Only*, gives this impression of Sam: "From a distance he is just another curly-haired Southerner, medium height, fair-haired. . . .

Get near to [him] and you feel at once his magnetic personality . . . his happy faith and contentedness."

Some of Sam's close friends coined the phrase "People are more important than things." These words became an axiom of Calvary policy, and a great many people happily welcomed the personal emphasis so apparent in his new program. There were always the few who shied away, not wishing to enter into a personal involvement, but they proved to be a dwindling minority.

In an account in *The Calvary Evangel*, the parish magazine, Shoemaker is quoted as announcing in his very first church service that all who cared to do so would be welcome to gather together once a week in the rectory for the single purpose of praying for spiritual revival at Gramercy Park. A few daring souls met the Wednesday after his first sermon. In the early autumn, a series of men's meetings commenced, and the number of those who wished to consider the implications of Shoemaker's major premise— "Christianity is a religion that works"—increased steadily. It was necessary to take over the rector's huge study as a meeting place. The high hopes of those who had selected Sam were quickly justified, and the rebirth of Calvary Church was an apparent fact.

After but a few more weeks in his new post, Sam reported in *The Evangel:* "My days have been filled with personal interviews, sometimes three or four a day, and lasting from half-an-hour to several hours." In most of his sermons he used the stories of those who had come along and been helped. One of the very first individuals to catch fire proved to be a handsome, but poorly educated "east-sider" named Charlie, a young Italian. Very early every day he would deliver morning newspapers along Third Avenue and his route included Gramercy Park. Since the new rector of Calvary was an early riser, not much time elapsed before the man and the newsboy met. To meet Sam often led to a warm friendship, and such was the case here. As Charlie rarely saw other residents in the Park face to face, the rector easily became his favorite customer.

One morning, as the two chatted in the rectory hallway, "it" happened. No one knows what the rector said on that occasion but new life came to Charlie, and those who heard about Charlie's prayer could never forget it. It was a classic, a simple plea in nine words: "God, manage me, 'cause I can't manage myself."

Individual lives continued to be changed. Harvie Z., an unattractive undergraduate recently dismissed from Dartmouth, had seemingly little to offer. He was a young Jew with generally nervous mannerisms, shifty eyes, and a skin blotched with acne—a young man without any apparent goal in life. But a month after meeting Shoemaker he had become a composed, friendly chap who walked with a brisk gait and a "I-know-where-I'm-going" style. His face radiated the change which had taken place within. An onlooker might have asked, "What's going on here?" And that would have been an extremely good question, for much *had* happened, much that was of a spiritually revolutionary quality.

There must have been many parts of this young fellow's story which were acutely negative, for it was a sordid tale of wasted years. Harvie surely found the retelling of such incidents as his expulsion from college agonizingly painful, and his mentor, as many of us discovered, never minced matters, rarely left a stone unturned. What was equally important, Sam Shoemaker never seemed shocked. In this instance, the light began to break when the "patient" suddenly realized that his dishonesties and self-indulgences could be entirely erased, and not because he really deserved a new chance.

Does this not form the crux of the Christian message— forgiveness that operates like one of those damp cloths we have all used at a blackboard, which quickly cleans the background of its white crosses, dashes, figures, and words, and leaves it ready to be written on again? When I eventually met Harvie, he had become a theology student. I observed a very gracious young man, endowed with great mental sharpness and, above all, possessing a perfectly delightful, uninhibited sense of humor. I simply couldn't picture him as the individual he told us he had been.

A third younger man to be reached during Shoemaker's first year at Calvary was Jim Smith who had been an avid critic of Sam at Princeton. Jim had decided he wanted no part of this self-denying philosophy of life that he heard Sam talk about. Privileged young fellows like Jim secretly feared the challenge of a personal interview with Sam and preferred their comforts and independence to an adventure into the unknown.

While college authorities in general seemed to assume that undergraduates had few if any problems, Shoemaker knew all too well the divided life many of them were leading. Sam made it clear that, if he were to help a student, he expected a specific experience to take place where the student might see himself in the light of Christ's perfection, or seriously consider seeking God's particular will for his vocation.

As a way out for himself, Jim formed the practice of talking quite glibly about "this guy Shoemaker who wants everyone to go into the ministry." Such a line was partially justified because Sam did have an intense desire to see more men, especially campus leaders, go to theology school, and at times he may have pressed too hard.

The interesting thing in this particular case is that, when Jim graduated and left the security of his campus life, it was Sam Shoemaker to whom he decided to look for advice. Actually Jim's choice of vocation had backfired, and when he didn't know which way to turn, in desperation one hot Saturday afternoon he found himself on his way to Gramercy Park. The old rectory looked grim. After pacing back and forth, he gathered sufficient courage to give the doorbell a good push, still half hoping no one would answer. However, in a moment, there stood the very man, about whom for so many months he had been critical, ready to welcome him.

"Come in, come in. . . . No, not busy at all. Terribly glad to see you!"

So in Jim went, and in no time the two were sitting in Shoemaker's study, talking and laughing. One would have thought that the young rector had all the time in the world, and for an occasion like this, he did. Availability was one of the secrets of Sam's success.

*   *   *

It was the blossoming of the mid-week activities at Calvary which attracted my own interest. After a year or so, it became known through the press that something very special, perhaps unique, was happening on Gramercy Park. Every Thursday evening, lay men and women of all sorts were speaking briefly from their own experiences of what God was doing in their lives.

I was on the staff of a church a mere forty blocks further uptown from Calvary and felt a keen desire to see at firsthand what these meetings were like. The first thing that struck me was the manner in which Sam was personally involved. Quite obviously he was giving himself as fully to these gatherings as he was to his Sunday services and personal counseling. I watched him as he greeted people; moderated most of the gatherings; lingered afterwards, making himself available to strangers; speaking to anyone who might have been moved by what had been said and wanted to talk. I noticed the little red book in which he was invariably jotting down appointments for follow-up. I was intrigued, and so continued to visit Gramercy Park, always especially interested in the panel of speakers who had recently found spiritual renewal, or new direction, about which they spoke so openly.

On my fourth visit, I had a healthy surprise. A husband and wife took about fifteen minutes to speak and, at more than one point, so naïve and touching had been their recent discoveries that as they spoke the rafters fairly shook from the laughter. Shoemaker was a master at quickly reviewing and pointing up such stories. As they finished, he chimed in: "Bill here saw God's spirit alive in others like himself, faced the false, self-defeating security of drinking, and, like a child trusting an older person, asked God to take over. It worked." The crowd registered their approval.

A quiet pause followed. Then, "Let's hear from a few others who have been seeing God at work in these meetings," Sam went on.

Another pause and then an alarming query arose within myself: *Was it time for me to say why I was coming here?* God forbid! But our genial host now seemed to be looking straight at me. "Yes, come along," I heard him say, to my horror. "Tell us who you are and then what you've been thinking, sitting here these past Thursday nights."

The platform on which the moderator sat seemed a mile high. As I walked toward it, I felt nothing so much as a wild desire to run. Half to the moderator and half to the audience I turned and stammered, "Really, I can't think of a thing to say. My mind is a blank, my heart is pounding, and I feel like a schoolgirl making her maiden speech."

"Fine, fine," encouraged our host, as a wave of laughter ran across the room. "But tell us what brings you back."

"It's really quite simple," I replied. "I've been watching some marvelous things happen in people's lives. The sense of confusion about my own work has also disappeared. I realize how effectively God can use the average person, and what a potent power for good can come from those who are willing to speak the word of faith and be honest about their own personal discoveries. Well, I guess I want to be a part."

In the end, it was a number of similar experiences which more than anything else lifted me above denominational barriers and eventually made me a member of the Calvary staff myself.

This explosion of new life at Calvary Church, in terms of the number of new faces and increased vitality per capita, eventually made the old rectory totally inadequate. Sam Shoemaker saw what had to be done and secretly had an architect work on plans for an eight-story replacement, Calvary House. The creation of this unusual parish house was a major venture and it had a humorous side, for when Sam Shoemaker accepted the vestry's call, he had done so with the express understanding that he would never be asked to engage in any kind of a building program.

3 /

People and Pulpit:
Sam Shoemaker's Work—I

*T*o understand Sam Shoemaker's power in the pulpit one must first realize his great talent as a writer.

In the last letter I received from him, shortly before his death, was this significant paragraph: "I realize how long ago many factors entered into my writing. When I was a child, I used to go in and peck at the old Underwood in my Father's office, and while I was still very young indeed, he gave me a good Underwood that I used for years. Just this little piece of machinery was a spur to writing more. Then all the time at Princeton, with [Professor] Bobby Root and the rest, I can see the hand of God in it all, that the most I could do *included writing*."

From the beginning of his ministry at Calvary, he would devote Wednesday or Thursday morning to the composition of his Sunday sermon. I can see him now pounding out with zest these weekly masterpieces on an old Corona. The entire talk would be done well inside of three hours and what so many clergymen made too technical or too profound he was able to express in the clearest, most concise way. He was fond of following the homely advice of a country parson near his home in Maryland: "Don't put the hay too high. Spread it on the ground where both the giraffes and jackasses can get it!" And this he usually achieved, even in dealing with subjects like spiritual healing or immortality, or in focusing on the miracles of Jesus and great mysteries like the resurrection. His masterful use of English, his orderliness of thought, and his simple examples from everyday life created sermons that everyone could both comprehend and take to heart.

Interruptions rarely bothered him. He would be typing away when a gentle tap on his study door would indicate that his secretary, or his wife, or one of us who later helped lift the load of his paperwork as it grew heavier, had something which seemed important for him to know. A hearty "Come in" would invariably ring out and, except on those rare occasions when he felt clearly that the intrusion was unnecessary or especially inconvenient, he would lean back in his swivel chair, smiling, and listen with kind attention to what had to be said. Then with his thanks, or a brief word of advice, he would turn back to the little battered machine and proceed to hammer away without a moment's hesitation.

Or, again, the 'phone would ring, the girl at the switchboard having clear instructions to put through all incoming calls. "Yes," he would say in a tone communicating sincere interest, and with never a trace of irritation, he would talk for a moment, or occasionally at considerable length, and on hanging up, turn again to his work without a sign of having been distracted. He might even pull a card or two from his index box of special quotations and rapidly type off words he had decided to use long before the telephone conversation took place.

There was scarcely a correction on his typed sheets, so easily did his thoughts express themselves through his finger tips. In fact we used to smile, ruefully, in later days when we came to use regularly one of these sermons in each issue of *The Evangel* or the *Faith-at-Work* magazine. A special receptacle in the editorial office preserved copies of each of his talks in the chronological order in which they were given, and it was not always easy to select, out of four or five, the one we thought would be most appropriate for the next issue of the magazine. But the real trouble the assistant editor and I faced came from our need to chisel out four or five hundred words, so that even Sam Shoemaker's contributions would not take more than five pages, our outside limit on everything we printed. So beautifully were the sermons phrased and so cohesive that not a little patience and time invariably went into their condensation and preparation for the printer.

As for the preacher's delivery, while perhaps secondary, this can also only be described in superlative terms such as "most impressive." Sam Shoemaker had a superb speaking voice, and his slight southern accent only made it the more agreeable. His clear enunciation and almost complete lack of gesticulation made for easy listening and attention.

To all outward appearances he was speaking from memory with complete spontaneity. Few newcomers in his congregations realized that actually he had a clear, double-spaced manuscript on the pulpit before him, or that, as he proceeded, he regularly slipped from top to bottom each sheet as it was used. He never seemed to be glancing down at an outline or notes, and many, though they heard him regularly, disputed the fact that he was actually reading his sermons. Or, *was* he? So well were the contents of each talk fixed in his mind, and so fluent were his thoughts, that he appeared entirely free from the lectern and I could never quite decide in my own mind whether "reading" was the correct description of his delivery. In a sense it didn't matter.

When I once questioned him on the need of his typing out the sermons so carefully and suggested that he might save time and strength by speaking from notes, he cut me off abruptly. "Not a bit of it," he said. "Let me use my own method. I know my limitations." And that was that.

What did he talk about? The Person of Jesus Christ formed the subject of perhaps every fourth or fifth sermon. And the nature and work of the Holy Spirit, "the forgotten Person of the Trinity," was the subject of many more. He had magnificent talks focused on the festivals of Christmas and Easter, which were profoundly perceptive and theologically revealing. But more than all else, he was concerned with the practical aspects of faith, and faith related to daily life, and he continued to keep a personal note central in his message. He believed with his whole soul that Christianity worked, and he ached to get nominal church members as well as pagans to try it.

Furthermore, his appeal was never to men's desire to succeed, or to the possibilities of self-advancement, or even self-realization. He constantly underlined the supernatural aspects of Christianity and strongly advocated that people dedicate their natural gifts to their Creator, rather than seek opportunities for self-expression. To put this another way, his aim did not consist in urging people to "measure up to their best," or even abide by a high set of moral principles, much as he believed in these. His aim for the individual could only be expressed in words like "commitment" and "trust," a different, deeper approach than much of the popular preaching of the day.

Yet his challenge had nothing vague or theoretical about it. One sermon, which as time went on found its way into magazine and leaflet form and, at the time of his death, was still being reprinted by the thousands, has the simple title "Three Levels of Life." As an explanatory subhead it put the question, "Do You Live by Instinct, Conscience, or Grace?" Nothing could have been simpler, less sensational or more devastating in its condemnation of one's selfishness and pride. It concluded:

"There are not two categories of people: those who do what they want, and those who do what they should. There are *three*: and the third consists of those who have been made new by Jesus Christ, and in whom what they want to do and what they ought to do are one and the same thing. These are the Spirit-led people, who are the happiest, most lovable, and most creative people in the world."

The Scriptures formed the basis of Sam Shoemaker's preaching. He was a "Bible Christian." But, as has been intimated, he felt he should pitch his message to challenge—and where possible to cure—the mounting evil he saw both in individuals and on the world scene around him. World War I had given rise to Communism and also left as an aftermath a widespread disintegration in individuals. The Jazz Age was flourishing in America, while servicemen who were unable to get home and thousands of others exploded with reckless gaiety overseas. Shoemaker sought to present a Christian message vital enough to challenge both materialism and immorality.

Beyond the faith of his fathers and his studies, he had at hand the all too rare experience of Christian teamwork, resulting from the time he had spent traveling and working with group friends. He encouraged one of these, the Reverend Sherwood S. Day, to outline the primary New Testament principles which they had learned to accept together and which had come to form a central part in his own credo. In one of the 1926 issues of *The Calvary Evangel* "Sherry" summed up these convictions as follows:

(1) **God guidance.** By "guidance" is meant communion with the living God. . . . "Listening to God" and "two-way prayer" are phrases often used in speaking of this experience. In "listening to

God" the general movement is from God to man, not from man to God, a movement distinctive of Christianity . . . and quite different from the tragic effort, described in so many faiths, of man's attempts to climb into the presence of God. "Guidance" is simply the experience of God flooding into a man's life to give him direction and power.

(2) **Fearless dealing with sin.** Whether or not we like the word sin, few today would deny that all is not well with mankind. We know this to be true among ourselves; we are so often "divided, inferior, and unhappy" when we long to be "united, superior, and happy." All too often something within us flares up in anger, or passion, or utter selfishness and perhaps makes us afraid of the future. What is wrong? The Bible calls it sin, and the simplest definition of sin that I know is "anything that separates me from God or from another person." The Bible frankly faces the fact of sin but does not stop there. It offers a cure. Jesus Christ took men exactly where they were. He faced them honestly and fearlessly with the facts and gave them the courage to do the same with themselves, and then showed them the way out.

(3) **Openness,** or "sharing." By this is meant confession— willingness to be honest about one's sins and failures. "Confess your faults one to another" is the admonition of our Lord's brother, the Apostle James. Confession to God alone is often not good enough, for it costs nothing and may merely amount to being honest to a subjective picture of God which one has built up for oneself. This involves no real repentance and usually is an easy way of trying to ease one's conscience. Besides, openness is often necessary if we are to help others. It establishes confidence for it reveals the fact that the Christian who seeks to be redemptive has been through experiences not unlike those of the one he seeks to help. This is also sound pedagogy for knowing that all men fall short of their aspirations, we start with what is known, we start where people are, and thus put the known ahead of the unknown. Christ may be known to only a few, but sin, failure, and longing are known to all.

(4) **The necessity of adequate expressional activity.** I believe that there is no vital, sustained experience of Jesus Christ where there is not active expressional activity. In other words no high level of contagious spiritual life can be maintained without trying to pass that life on to others. A person may be very busy in

good works and have practically no spiritual impact on the people he sees or works with, or in the situations in which he labors. Actually, we all come to know God the better as we share Him with others. A spiritual experience, however rich, which is not given away dies or becomes abnormal. This is the reason for a type of very pious but very unattractive Christian who constantly tries to superimpose his will and way on others. For such, religion is more often a hobby than a life.

(5) **Stewardship.** The New Testament teaches that life is a whole and cannot be divided into compartments such as "sacred" or "secular." When we surrender ourselves to God in Christ, we acknowledge that He who "bought us with a price" owns us and all that He has entrusted us with. On such a basis, houses, lands, money, relationships, all we are and have, make up a trust. All sense of possessiveness must go. Our trust is to be administered under the guidance of the Holy Spirit. This principle of stewardship gives the lie to a materialistic heresy abroad today to the effect that wealth is intrinsically evil and poverty is of itself virtuous. The Gospel does not teach that, but rather that all belongs to God—not merely a tenth or even nine-tenths, but all.

(6) **Teamwork.** Jesus Christ practiced teamwork. He gathered a small group of workers about Him and in this respect set an example for His followers. He believed that the highest light for the individual is to be found in association with others, in the group, in His church. When His followers were "of one mind, of one accord, in one place," the Spirit came. His teachings emphasized corporate life; the individual was to play his all-important part in a well-coordinated whole.

How often today we fail to raise up such leadership! Few Christian leaders will pay the price and undergo the pain of developing other leaders and carrying them to the place where they in turn are able to train others. Furthermore, truth itself is presented more adequately through a group than through an individual. A united front, made up of individuals of varied personalities who give the same message but from different points of view, carries unusual conviction in situations where a single individual may not appeal.

(7) **Loyalty.** The supreme loyalty in life should, of course, be to Jesus Christ, but that loyalty involves lesser loyalties. The person or group of persons embodying for us the highest challenge we know, the person or persons who have been used to reveal Jesus

Christ to us, are persons or groups demanding our loyalty. Loyalty in the abstract and loyalty in the concrete are two very different things. One knows churches, educational institutions, and individuals who assert loyalty to Christ but see no need to be loyal to individuals who are incarnating His teachings. It was said of the first Christians, "See how they love one another."

4/

Pen and Publications:
Sam Shoemaker's Work—II

Calvary Church had been shorn of its twin towers at the time New York City built its first subway, known as the Lexington Avenue Line. But though these changes gave the brownstone building a rather squat appearance, its prominent location on Fourth Avenue and its friendly main entrance naturally remained the same.

It was through these portals that Shoemaker welcomed a multitude of worshippers—the regular members of Calvary parish increasingly augmented by inquirers of diverse backgrounds, some of whom had no church affiliations at all. It made no difference. The rector always sought to relate people back to the denominations in which they had grown up, and his first concern was to make it clear that the new Calvary program sought to meet individuals at their points of need and was carried on above any divisions of party, class, or color.

A few parish organizations languished, failing to fulfill what he felt to be primary needs, but in the main the work of the local church gained steadily in numbers and strength. Episcopal quotas and assessments were regularly met and frequently surpassed. The elderly and infirm were visited, inmates of nearby hospitals and prisons cared for, and budgets balanced. Sam Shoemaker was out to build up the Body of Christ locally and at the same time extend His worldwide Kingdom by every possible means. His zest kindled members' enthusiasm. His imagination surprised people, many of whom joyfully acclaimed his proposed plans as if they had long been waiting for the church to take exactly the lead which he was indicating.

He was particularly anxious to create a strong staff. He placed no limit on the number of his full-time fellow workers, and he had the optimistic view that some able assistants might participate with him on a volunteer basis. And, believe it or not, it worked. Mrs. Paul Revere Reynolds, the wife of a New York businessman, was one of the first volunteers. She had found a new quality of life in a few personal talks with the rector, and the results seemed to her too good to be true. She shortly published a book, *New Lives for Old*, about the experience she and others had found, and like Isaiah of old she turned up one day in the spirit of "Here am I. Send me." She was the first to call the vestry's attention to the number of young office workers who were passing their old building during the business week. A series of noonday services was arranged for those living or working in the neighborhood, and a brand new notice board was erected on the corner to apprise passersby that they would be foolish to miss the new, free events which the old church now had to offer.

She went further, this woman who got things done! Among the advertising cards in the old Fourth Avenue trolley cars appeared one with the picture of a handsome young clergyman who, it was said, not only conducted the services at Calvary Church but held weekly meetings in his rectory. Here business and professional people were speaking regularly from their own experience, telling what faith in God could do to answer daily problems, and also how to find it. No one could have estimated the number of individuals whose attention was arrested by those cards. But of the many who were caught, so to speak, was Miss Olive M. Jones, a past president of the National Education Association. Olive had no church home but desperately needed one. Most important she needed the good news of forgiveness and life which Sam Shoemaker had to give her. She, too, found that "it worked," and on retirement from her job as principal of "the bad boys' school" of New York, she also joined Sam's staff. In fact when Calvary House arose in the place of the old rectory, the new building, which provided both staff quarters and overnight accommodations for visitors, was presided over by Olive Jones as director. It was she also who composed a new curriculum for the church school for children, and who, with the aid of a number of fellow staffers, preëminently Horace Lukens, and then Claxton and Vicky Monro, built up the children and youth work at Calvary in a way never attempted before.

Certainly, of the many other parts of the program, those relating to Calvary Mission, operated by Harry Hadley on East Twenty-third Street, and the Thursday evening meetings at 61 Gramercy Park attracted the most attention and brought results most highly prized by the rector. Here is his own description of the remarkable growth of the open weekly meetings at Gramercy Park.

"When we began the Thursday Evening Group we asked those persons to come who wanted to learn how to reach others, one by one, for the living God. . . . The first comers were, therefore, principally Christians of some years' experience who had never learned how to witness, or else those who had recently begun their religious experiences and wished to impart it, when they could, to those who did not know God. But into it have been brought not only Christians who wanted to know the procedure of personal work but completely new people as well, some with no belief or spiritual experience whatever. . . .

"I am convinced that the average Christian worker thinks in too advanced terms for ordinary people, and that we are missing the needs of the unconvinced precisely because we do not know how to turn back to the early stages of conviction. We tend to take people for granted, to assume things which are not so, to skip over necessary steps in development.

"So it becomes inevitable that a group must be a medium for the discussion of all the varieties of personal religious experience. . . . There is about it all a gaiety and gladness, not professional, not put on, but spontaneous and understanding. Anything may happen. People come, bound they will not say a word, and something in the atmosphere coaxes their opinions out of them. There is the utmost freedom. . . .

"These people are from every denomination and church. Some are church-workers, some are agnostics at the beginning. Many have literally found God simply by being present.

"I have always tried to make it clear that this group was in no sense connected with Calvary Church and its people, for I have never wanted it to be thought that we are trying to boom this parish. We simply want to help as many people as possible in every church to learn how to witness effectively for Christ. It is an interesting experience to see an out-and-out worldling and a quiet church-worker discover one another, find something in common, learn that each is human with weaknesses and aspirations much alike— and go away with prejudices exploded. There is literally every kind of human being here, elderly women and young men, lots of them—business people and deaconesses, social workers and artists. It is a real cross section. A cultivated voice will be followed by one that murders the King's English—and we are hardly conscious of it, so completely have the walls been taken down between the groups which superficial life marks off for us. There has been a lot of sentimental rot about being 'all one in Jesus Christ.' I have heard it on the lips of snobs and scamps who hide behind it to conceal their own unbrotherliness. But it is a reality here. And everyone who comes feels it."

Quite a report! Quite a meeting! So, as Calvary's program developed, two interesting points became ever more apparent: (1) Here was a place to learn the how of faith, both in sermons and in groups—How to find God. How to pray. How to read the Bible. How to pass faith on. And (2) much of the *how* flowed straight from the fellowship itself and a quality of life which is centered, not in individual hopes or even in personal vocations but in that supernatural Other, and is seen and understood—one might almost say absorbed—in the very process of participating in God's work and worship.

This work was like a newly launched ship. Never was there any question as to who stood at the helm, but a sturdy crew or team was ever aiding and abetting, and with this body of teammates who made up a veritable spiritual family came strength and impact and thoroughness.

Later, in World War II, Winston Churchill underlined this necessity for a team when, in refuting those who criticized the first cross-channel attacks on occupied France, at Dieppe, as being too costly in lost lives, he wrote: "Above all it was shown that individual skill and gallantry. . . would not prevail, and that teamwork was the secret of success." His inference was that the tragic loss had been more than justified by the valuable lesson learned.

Applying Jesus' own conception of the Kingdom of God as a realm of right relationships, and relying on His promise that "where two or three had gathered in His name" he would be actively present, the Calvary staff and their friends then initiated more and more informal meetings, not a few for their own growth and planning, and many others to welcome beginners and strangers. One was a men's meeting whose size and make-up offered the informality which evoked participation.

One spring someone on the larger team presented the staff with the breathtaking idea of taking the Thursday night meetings out-of-doors to the famous area, three blocks away, known as Madison Square. A steady deterioration had taken place there since the era of the Jerome Mansion and Delmonico's Restaurant, and the later period when Madison Square Garden had been the amusement center of the city. The Square still offered ample open space with an abundance of shade trees and park benches, and had become the refuge of idlers and a convenient place for the inhabitants of numerous midtown rooming houses to exercise in a mild way and take the air. Now its comparative quiet was to be challenged on Sunday evenings, as the plan suggested, by a procession consisting of Calvary Church's white-vested choir, headed by one or two of the clergy, and augmented by a small group of selected lay men and women who were to speak in the same vein of personal testimony as that heard in the Thursday meetings.

None of the participants found it a particularly easy performance, and most of the speakers admitted experiencing self-consciousness bordering on terror. But, once again, Shoemaker waxed most enthusiastic and the meetings proved highly successful from the very start. After a few familiar hymns the speakers each took seven or eight minutes in which to tell their personal story, and before the closing prayer a warm invitation was extended to everyone present to follow the choir back to the church for a brief worship service.

One among the group of listeners who gathered from the adjacent benches on a certain June evening was Horace Howard, an electrician who was out of work and in despair as to where to turn for food for his wife and himself and their young baby, all of whom were existing in a one-room "walk-up" in a dilapidated building nearby. It was not difficult for Horace to be attracted to a diversion like this outdoor meeting or to follow the procession back to the church when the speaking was over. Though a Roman Catholic, he liked everything he saw and heard, and he felt impressed by the simple sincerity of those who had taken part. Sitting in the rear of the church, he again felt strangely warmed by what he heard, and so he lingered for a chat with one of the ministers. Later that night he returned to his rather squalid room with a dollar in his pocket and a quart of milk from the delicatessen. Equally important, he had discovered a few friends who offered immediate help both material and spiritual. In the years ahead, rehabilitated and working again, he became more active than before in his own church, and at the same time continued a close intimacy with the Calvary staff, some of whom he thought of as his spiritual family.

Before long, reports of these rather novel Madison Square meetings appeared in New York newspapers and brought another kind of inquirer from further afield. Among those who read and came to investigate was a sturdy son of Kansas who was on a sight-seeing trip to New York. He thought it would be a circus to see an Episcopal choir lined up on the curb of Twenty-third Street and to listen to Christians fanatical enough to speak of their faith from a soap box in the open air. Being a clergyman merely heightened his interest, and also led to his disguising his identity to the extent of wearing a bright red tie. But any tendency to hold aloof, or to make fun of the affair, quickly disappeared in the face of the speakers' sincerity and the quality of their messages. J. Herbert Smith had thus far done very well in the ministry and, among other accomplishments, had to his credit the erection of a new Episcopal church in his home diocese. But within a few minutes of his joining the crowd at the meeting in the park, he realized that he was listening to fellow Christians whose freedom and sense of purpose far exceeded his own. One girl from a home of privilege, who had moved personally from being an agnostic to being a believer who wanted to spend her life serving Jesus Christ, especially touched him by her simple story—that of a person whose empty life had been filled with joy and power. "Jack," like Horace Howard, decided to accept the invitation to return to the church for the service. This was followed in the ensuing days by several talks with Sam Shoemaker, whose associate minister he eventually became. As for the woman whose eloquent witness had first impressed him, it was she who a year or two later became his wife.

As the momentum increased, Calvary's new program added up to a many-sided successful experiment. Shoemaker held regular staff meetings to clear details and delegate responsibility but also so that he and his colleagues might acquire vision and gain power.

His instinct for leadership was augmented by the guidance of the Spirit. He expected those who worked with him to catch on without much instruction from himself. He suggested, encouraged, initiated, but definitely did not belabor the work with theory and exhortation.

Speaking personally, in the thirty and more years I had the opportunity of working with him, I remember Sam Shoemaker giving no lectures and little detailed instruction to those of us who made up his staff. We learned by doing, as we saw and were impressed by the pattern he himself followed. Special times for instruction rarely took place. Such wisdom as we acquired came to us in our stride as we were carrying out our plans together.

Naturally, instances occurred when, as rector, he offered specific advice by way of a "corrective," such as the day after a large meeting when he rather crossly suggested that I stop seeming to "dance attendance" on members of the fairer sex. At other times he might tell an amusing story on himself, usually about his own ineptness. But for the most part, the manner in which he tackled his job, plus some brief comment on current projects, brought the clarity and the truth we younger people needed.

During a year when I was acting specifically as a kind of executive secretary, keeping matters which seemed of prime importance on the top of the mass of papers which everlastingly accumulated on his desk, he arrived in his study about nine o'clock one Sunday evening, straight from an out-of-town speaking engagement. As usual I was on hand, fussing over letters and other material which seemed especially urgent.

"Oh, don't let's bother with all that tonight," he began.

HARRIS (defensively): "I'm just putting the most important stuff on top. . . . Here's a cable, and also a couple of special delivery letters from friends of yours."

SHOEMAKER: "No, no. Let all that go 'till the morning. You look as tired as I feel. There are times when one shouldn't scan a single line, however urgent. Other times, of course, when dictating thirty letters should seem most important, they're almost child's play. Pick and choose. The Lord will guide you."

What an answer to pressure! What an antidote to tension!

5 /

Calvary Church Reaches Out

*A*s the news spread and an ever-increasing number of visitors looked in on what was happening at Calvary, various church groups in Long Island, Westchester, and New Jersey asked for help. It was all right for them to come to Gramercy Park, but what about Gramercy Park coming to them?

One way in which Sam Shoemaker responded was to summarize his program in a sermon, "A Fourfold Plan for Spiritual Advance." This was taken from *The Evangel* and reprinted in the paperback *Creating Christian Cells,* which was also issued under the title *Groups That Work.* Here is a digest of what he wrote:

"There are four fundamental and universal factors in what we can call a Christian program . . . and the first is *Conversion.* This act is the turning of our lives over to God through Christ and surrender to Him. To all people in all ages who have in any thorough way become Christians, there has been a turning point, a place of departure from the old life and beginning of the new. The reason why so many of us grow so slowly or never really grow at all, is that we camouflage our sins, point to those of others as being greater, excuse our sins by pointing out our virtues, and will not be specific about exactly the 'nature of our wrongs.' And if we are on the whole decent and respectable folk, how about our spiritual ineffectiveness in making faith real to others as one sin? A man told me once his friends couldn't make him drunk, but neither could he make them sober. Is that sin, too?

"We are converted *from* sin *to* God. God is only an ideal to some, only a high name. Begin where you are. Be honest about your needs. The great need is for Someone to help. Is there anyone else but God? You can't do it by will power . . . for it needs supernatural grace.

"The second step is *Prayer*. This is lengthened conversation—the seeking of God's will and plan—but not trying to persuade Him to adopt your will and plan. *Living* religion *is* prayer, and we need to learn to pray at all times about everything. Prayer becomes not requests so much as communion, cooperation. This is how we find new strength.

"And with prayer there are other ways such as *Bible study* by which to draw spiritual strength for the new life. The Bible becomes not so much a rule book as a kind of pasture where we feed, and it speaks to us daily when we take time for it.

"The church, too, forms another source of strength. When we seriously get into the Christian life, we come for worship and for fellowship with each other as a kind of refill. Especially through the Holy Communion do we find God coming to us with grace in His hands. In prayer we reach towards Him: in the sacraments He reaches down to us.

"The third step is *Fellowship*. It would never have occurred to the early Christians that one would call himself a Christian until he had been baptized. One is not only baptized into Christ, but into His family the church. If you have not found out that the Christian life is a profoundly corporate experience, you have little understood it.

"We need the friends we make in Christ to help us when we are down, and also to share with when the spiritual sun is shining. We need the corrective and perspective of the ages of the church's life. We need buildings that help us to concentrate on God. We may find Christ alone, but we can only truly "abide" in Him in His company. Worship is one of the greatest of all ways to build up faith and Christian life. The church offers both formal services and the informal gathering of small groups. Services may be so formal that they are not the best places for some to experience their first exposure to Christ; the smaller, more informal company may be better—places where we can become familiar with the various kinds of Christian experience, talk out our difficulties, ask questions, compare experiences.

"The fourth step is *Witness*. Christ told us we were to be His witnesses. He has no other hands and feet and voices in the world but His people. The early church burned like a fire and spread rapidly because of the contagion of its people. They found a Risen Christ, and they were excited about it. They couldn't keep quiet. They witnessed by what they were, by what they did, and by what they said. People saw a change in them—a change for the better—and they wanted this faith and new life for themselves.

"People who love God become contagious for God. You don't have to egg them on; they can't help doing it. They have an Unseen Friend and a power that is given them from above. They are not all great saints, but most of them are great enthusiasts. And they can't help talking about what interests them most. If what you love is horse racing, or clothes, or the stock market, or your grandchildren, that is what you'll talk about. If what you love is God in Christ, you will find ways to communicate that to other people."

*   *   *

Along with the printed word went out teams of Calvary-associated people. One of my own first commissions when I linked up with the Calvary staff was to shepherd a team of New York laymen to speak in a church on Staten Island. A stock broker and a real estate operator were among those who caught an early ferry with me one Sunday morning to cross The Narrows. We took the time usually devoted to the sermon—plus perhaps an extra quarter of an hour—in order to say, humbly, what God had been doing in our own lives.

Another team answered an urgent request from the pastor of a small Congregational church in a village not far from Bernardsville, New Jersey. This rural community, some thirty-five miles from New York, was typical, churchwise, of many larger towns. The church was functioning in a desultory, conventional way, with its activities mostly in the hands of a few older, conscientious members.

The minister who wrote us had visited 61 Gramercy Park, and I knew that though his church faced no serious problems he was not a happy man. His letter urged us to send out a small team some Sunday evening. "We want you for supper," he said. "And then I'll turn over the evening service which you can run in any way you want. I think we need some personal witness from a few live wires who can tell how faith has become real in their own lives. . . ."

It proved a friendly congregation with a corps of ladies who produced macaroni and cheese and homemade cakes on a wholesale basis. About eight o'clock our host arranged us in a semicircle around his pulpit, gave a short announcement expressing gratitude for our visit, and got in a rousing hymn or two before looking at me with a kind of quizzical take-it-from-here-brother expression.

We did our best: a school teacher, a couple of younger businessmen, a lawyer, and myself. We even raised a laugh or two but, in the main, the congregation sat attentive, curious, and very serious. We were to close with another assigned hymn, but before announcing this, I said how delighted any of us visitors would be to talk further with individuals after the benediction. "The night is young. We haven't got to rush off."

Actually many people lingered, and little knots of men and women formed in different parts of the sanctuary. Personally, I was happy to find myself in a front pew, chatting with a local high-school boy who had apparently liked some of what he had heard. But how very polite we were and how very inconsequential our conversation! I kept wondering what this boy was really like. Then I recalled, uncomfortably, the surprising amount of dishonesty which had crept into my life at his age and remembered how in college "white lies," anything to cover up deficiencies and make me "one of the boys," had become my stock-in-trade. Secretly I was afraid that if I mentioned things like this I would lose the respect of this very lad whom I wanted to help. Mine was a most indecisive attitude, but the minutes were ticking away. Suddenly I found myself saying, "You know, W__, it's not just church atten-dance and what we say and do at meetings like this on Sunday nights that count. I believe God is far more interested in what happens in our lives on Monday and Tuesday and straight through the week." I went on to give chapter and verse of specific in-stances of the way my habit of dishonesty had grown during my college years. "It got worse and worse until God took over," I said; and reluctantly I described the dishonest act I felt most ashamed of when, as chairman of a dance committee, I had slyly slipped a sizable roll of bills into my own pocket, instead of report-ing accurately our total income to the university authorities. "All to buy myself a corny fur coat," I concluded.

No question now but that I had my young friend's full interest. He looked at me in amazement. "Gee," he said, "I never thought religion had anything to do with things like that. . . . Why I'm cheatin' right now, every day. You see my father runs the general store here and I cheat him all the time, never thinkin' much about it, out of both time and money. . . . Wonder what I ought to do?"

"Well, I appreciate your frankness," I answered. "You'll get no advice from me, however, for I believe you'll know well enough what to do when you ask God about it, just as I did when I paid back the money I'd taken from the dance committee." I smiled encouragingly and said nothing further.

Came a pause. Then a beautiful smile broke across that boy's face. He stood up and stretched. "Thanks," he said. "Of course I know what to do. I'm goin' home and find the old man right now and tell him what the score is. We'll have quite a talk. . . . See you later." And he was gone.

I then talked to a number of others and eventually found myself back at the parsonage where a few of us had prayed together before the meeting. Now I was visiting alone with the minister. He said the usual things, but after awhile and seemingly apropos of nothing, he knocked the ashes out of his pipe, cleared his throat, and volunteered, "As for myself, I know that smoking constitutes a definite compromise; but I can't give it up. . . . And I might as well also admit there's a shady side to my life. For instance, when the church assembly meets in Atlantic City, I usually slip away from the meetings and waste my time in a burlesque show or a cheap movie. How's that for a simpleton? No wonder God doesn't use me more."

"Perhaps you need a new start," I suggested. "Surely you can't believe that, with all the power Almighty God has available for us, you really need to be hung up on an unimportant personal habit like smoking. You know very well God can deal with that."

My brother clergyman laughed, "You're right. He can. Let's pray about it."

We sat hugging an old-fashioned, pot-bellied stove, and without moving we simply bowed our heads.

"I'm just a fool," my friend began. "A sad shepherd of my flock, and I'm sorry, really sorry, tonight, about it all. I give you myself, again, Lord. I'm asking you, through Christ, to clean me up."

After that my few words of loving blessing were superfluous, but

I said them and I felt exceedingly close to this staunch but formerly very lonely man.

As we got up, the pastor uttered a deep sigh of relief, one that, as it turned out, marked a new chapter in his life.

It was a month or more before I visited the village again, but one day I drove through the town on my way to an appointment further south. As I parked in front of the village store, my young friend happened to glance through the glass of the store's front door. He came bounding out and, grabbing my arm, yelled, "Say, great! Come on in. I want to introduce you to my father."

A heartwarming meeting that; and besides the story of the open relationship between the father and son in the store, I heard tell of a new weekly group with the minister at the manse, and also about W__'s girl and what a new quality of life was meaning to her, and to W__ and her together.

I hadn't time to see the minister that day but I felt sure his old pipes had long since been consigned to the ash heap. As for the church, with a core of newly live, open folks at the center, I believed a new chapter had begun there too. Later on the minister did reappear at Gramercy Park, and the smile on his face alone announced that things were indeed different.

* * *

When he could find the time, Sam liked nothing better than to go out himself on a traveling team. On one famous trip he got as far as California and participated in the leadership of a conference at the Mission Inn in Riverside. The importance of this journey for him centered in what happened in the lives of a married couple named Sandy and Daisy. A handsome Scotsman with a line of amusing anecdotes a mile long, Sandy had been a moderately successful barrister in the old country and a pillar of the church. On the surface his wife and he appeared comfortable and happy; but among those who knew there was general agreement that their troubles were plentiful and in the main due to the simple fact that Sandy bent his elbow far too frequently.

There had come a chance to move to California. "Daisy's health will be better there," Sandy had avowed, comforting himself further with the thought that the United States had Prohibition at the time.

Like most people who try to run away from themselves, Sandy's and Daisy's problems had tagged along. Law evasion was a wide-spread American habit, and the flow of Scotch through Sandy's home continued as freely as ever. With indulgence on his side and a smoldering resentment on his wife's, grimness descended as dark as it ever had been in Auld Reekie.

Then Sam and the New York team arrived. Sam had been apprised of the situation in Sandy's and Daisy's home. His first step was a canny one. Introducing himself to Daisy by 'phone, he asked if she could offer a few days' hospitality to another Scotswoman who happened to be with him on the team. And so it was arranged. Ella Lee became a houseguest and for a day or two a pleasant time was had by all, Ella being quite aware that trouble marked both sides of the coin but biding her time and praying for wisdom.

Then one afternoon when the women were alone Daisy "asked for it" in a roundabout way over the tea table. The talk went like this:

"How good it's been to have you here, Ella! Of course I am sorry about Sandy but that's one of those things."

"Yes," said Ella, "it has been good. But somehow I'm not thinking of Sandy as much as I'm thinking of you."

"Me! Why, Ella, come now! Whatever have you in mind?"

"Ah, if you only wanted to face it and not defend yourself, I'd like nothing better than a chance to speak out."

"But you *have* the chance, my dear, always. Why should I feel anything but gratitude if you've a word of advice or see some way of helping us?"

A silence and then quietly Ella found the words. "It's not just robbing a bank or acquiring a self-indulgent habit that creates havoc in a home like yours. If you could but forget your husband's behavior—and forgive him—I believe you'd see that the self-pity and self-righteousness which has built up in your own mind are enough to drive any man to the bottle."

There it was, and despite her remarks Daisy didn't like it. Self-pity? Self-righteousness? How could anyone? And how justified she, Daisy, was to be indignant when day after day! . . . Then something happened, some clear picture of herself as a critical old woman broke in upon her. She realized for the first time just how directly she herself had contributed to the impasse.

Shaken, she admitted, "You're right, Ella. Yes, much as I hate to admit it, you've put your finger on the very spot where something can be done. I'll start with my own faults and leave dear Sandy to the Lord. I have become a crabbed old woman."

Ella kept as quiet as a mouse, so Daisy went on thinking. Then she smiled across her cup. "Will you pray with me? Will you let me tell God right here and now, with you, that I'm sorry, that I want to be different?"

The women bowed their heads while Daisy asked for help and Ella just gave thanks.

About a week later, Sandy found himself driving his wife to the weekend conference. Ella sat in the back seat and behind her with the luggage was Sandy's bag, replete with a couple of Agatha Christie paperbacks and two bottles of Scotch whiskey. "Now it's understood that I'm attending no meetings," Sandy repeated as they approached the hotel, and with a laugh Daisy answered, "You're to be as free as a bird."

But a strange experience lay ahead for the driver. What a delightful succession of people he met! How lonely he began to feel at meeting time, closeted alone in his room. Even Agatha and his liquid refreshment failed to ease his sense of emptiness. On the morning of the third day, he deliberately made a date for luncheon with Sam Shoemaker who he felt would understand. Still avoiding the meetings as he strolled about the grounds, he became aware of a surprising sense of expectancy.

At the luncheon table, he felt both the freedom he had wanted and also something else—the true and loving concern of the man who sat with him. They talked of all sorts of things "from birds and flowers to world events," as he used to express it in telling the story, later. And then the strangest thing happened. Over the apple pie he heard himself bluntly declaring, "I drink too much!"

"Bless your heart," answered Sam laughing. "We've known that for years. But the important question is what are you going to do about it?"

Sandy was ready. "Just exactly what my wife has done, I imagine. She's been so different this past week, our life has seemed like a second honeymoon."

When the two men left the dining room, it was to find a quiet place where they could pray. Sandy simply told God he was sorry and asked for another chance. According to Sam, he got it in double measure.

A new home emerged after Sandy and Daisy had put their lives under new management. Their correspondence to us in New York described it as a place where many, many others came for help, a place where both self-pity and self-indulgence, and every other block to the Spirit, went down the drain, a spot where many who needed fellowship found themselves in group meetings and also off on teams to other places in California to speak about the good news of the second chance.

*   *   *

Back at "61" I heard Sam talking one day about Jesus' phrase "fishing for men" which the Lord had used with his own friends so early in their discipleship. As usual, the rector told some stories about twice-born people like Sandy and Daisy. "I've been seeing again," he said, "that you don't approach trout with a hammer or try to grab any kind of fish by the lapel. Jesus once said be 'as wise as serpents.' There's strategy, there's humor, and there's love. When the right bait is offered with patience, the fish will take it."

6 /

The Breeze of the Spirit

*T*he opening of Calvary House, an impressive event in itself, had a spiritual significance which made it a milestone in Sam Shoemaker's ministry. Besides two assistant clergymen, he had now gathered, as a staff, some fourteen or fifteen lay people of various ages and backgrounds to carry forward the parish work of many kinds and, beyond this, to minister in a nondenominational spirit to anyone who looked to Calvary for help. This group of workers lived as a family, gathered under one roof, and had their meals together in a common dining room.

It was an exciting experience just to feel part of such a staff, and tions of all those involved. Each of us in our commitment to God had undertaken to become better acquainted with our Bibles and to devote more time to our prayers. Now, as part of a Christian community, we were encouraged to make these practices an adventure and, since our days were bursting with activity, the standard practice in the house was for its residents to rise early enough to establish a time for their private devotions before breakfast.

For me I discovered the enormous value of "classics" like Oswald Chambers' *My Utmost for His Highest* as a supplement to Bible study. Thomas Kelly's *Testament of Devotion, The Practice of the Presence of God* by Brother Lawrence, and Thomas à Kempis's *The Imitation of Christ* also proved of enormous help.

Under Olive Jones's leadership as the first director of the house, the program for both parish and ecumenical activities was then coordinated through a 9:00 A.M. meeting, five days a week, on the second floor of our new home. What a forthright, delightful moderator Olive turned out to be! She had the "breeze of the spirit," and she communicated the new quality of life she had found to those of us who met with her.

The emphasis always lay on worship and devotion rather than on planning, although there was plenty of discussion about the countless jobs which had to be done. First came the Bible, the reading of a few verses which had come to take on special meaning for the person who suggested them. This was followed by an unhurried time for meditation and waiting upon God when, as a family, we might claim Jesus' promise that, where two or three were gathered, there He would be in their midst. It was a remarkable experience, for as we waited, inwardly listening to the voice of the Spirit, there was no question but that we were renewed, often convicted of personal failure, inspired, and, in a very real measure, made one. It was both a privilege and a spiritual exercise to be on that team. Several of us found it helpful to make use of pencil and paper for recording the thoughts which came and listing the forthcoming work of the day. After the quiet, those who wished to pool their thoughts with the group as a whole had the chance to do so. And, finally, with a prayer or two of intercession, we broke up.

Of course one of the secrets of teamwork is personal openness, and opportunities were always available, sooner or later, for members of the staff to talk two by two, especially about the hang-ups or lack of understanding between themselves. And what a release would come as this personal sharing, some of it costly in terms of one's own pride, took place!

Norman Grubb, former general secretary of the Worldwide Evangelization Crusade, put this principle in a nutshell for us once by telling of an experience he went through in his work in Africa. He said: "When I was on a visit to Central Africa, I found myself among companies of African Christians, and some missionaries, who lived 'walking in the light' with each other. I had never before experienced such free, open, and happy fellowship; but it was completely honest. If jealousy, criticism, covetousness, impurity, coldness of heart had a hold on anyone, as they met together they would quietly say so, and praise would ascend from all for Jesus' cleansing. I was often smitten in heart that the same kind of things went on within me—but I was not *saying* so.

"Then one day a man I had met in England and had disliked

arrived unexpectedly. He gave me a warm greeting and I gave him the same; but in a second the Spirit said to me, 'You hypocrite; you know you don't mean that!'

"I recognized my sin of dislike and hypocrisy and confessed it in secret to God. But did I get rid of it that way? Indeed not. Every time I saw him, I felt the same toward him. Then God showed me that my repentance was not genuine: I wanted to repent in secret and save my face in public. My respectability meant more to me than the fact that I had sinned and needed cleansing. I had to tell the man right out; and, as a member of that Christian company, to be really honest I had to tell them all. It took me two days to do that. I learned how deep inward pride is. But when I 'broke' and did it, in a moment the antagonism was gone. And I began to see the reality and release of walking in the light, for myself and for the fellowship."

I had much to learn along this same line. As a Presbyterian I had theoretically no special disagreements with my Episcopal team-mates, who outnumbered me. But secretly I felt ruffled by two or three who kept harping, it seemed to me, on the value of taking communion every day. In my own church I had been in the habit of preparing for the "Lord's Supper" by certain well-established customs, such as attending a preparatory lecture which was held the Friday preceding the Sunday service. And besides, in our denomination the Lord's Supper was only administered four or five times during the year. What a relief to talk the whole question through with one of the strongest advocates of daily communion with whom I had been estranged! A barrier had separated us. His convictions about the bread and the wine, "the elements," varied greatly from mine. In a sense we were both right, like two men correctly describing the opposite sides of the same coin; but our silence and suspicion had been wrong. Now neither of us felt compelled to abandon our beliefs, but we understood each other and, what was more important, felt a most loving appreciation for what we did respectively believe.

* * *

The staff itself was made up of many small teams and often the work we had to do was assigned to such a team. For instance, as the inquiries increased and more and more letters came in asking about what was taking place at 61 Gramercy Park, three of us volunteered to answer these. One of this team was a man experienced in letter-writing, and two women were secretaries. We felt that each incoming letter represented an opportunity to help someone. We explained the simple, rewarding step of turning one's life over to God, invited those within reach to look in at an open meeting at Calvary House, and furnished names and addresses of Calvary friends who could be contacted in various sections of the country. Dozens of "pen pals" resulted, as well as quite a number of book buyers and subscribers to *The Evangel*.

Another team ran the magazine, and still another sold books, while several groups sprang up to make it easy for office and business people to enjoy fellowship at an hour convenient to them. Out of one businessmen's group came Ebby Thatcher who, as we shall see in the next chapter, heard the good news that a spiritual answer to alcoholism existed and promptly relayed this to Bill Wilson. A little later a midweek communion service added prayers for the healing of the sick, with the laying on of hands for those who wished it. Still later, as will be described in a special chapter, a vital laymen's group sprang up under the moderatorship of "Red Cap 42" at Grand Central Station.

After our marriage, my wife and I took an apartment some ten blocks south of Gramercy Park and, quite unexpectedly, a cell started there over a coffee pot. We wanted to see and talk with an old friend but lacked the time and strength to provide him with a company dinner, so we asked him to come along just for a cup of coffee. The evening proved profitable as well as hilarious. On the way out he allowed as how he might repeat the visit the following week. As I remember it, he next turned up with a friend and again so much happened that we decided it would be fun to have the coffee pot "perking" on that evening every week.

Over the months this group expanded to a round dozen and became immersed in studying and discussing leadership training, with a special emphasis on evangelism. At the end of a little over a year, the conviction came to several that this apartment group should become responsible periodically for a large, open witness meeting in the Great Hall at Calvary. Sam Shoemaker expressed enthusiasm, so with his approval we arranged a monthly gathering, very much like the original midweek meetings in the old rectory to which the public were invited to hear a panel of business and professional men and women speak out of their own experience about a "faith that works." In due time this group, augmented three times a year by leaders from other sections of the country and from Canada, held a yearly spring conference, first at Gramercy Park and then, after Sam Shoemaker had taken a church in Pittsburgh, in the Pocono Mountains. But we are moving ahead of our story.

It became clear that at Calvary House we were meeting and dealing with people as Jesus did in three ways. The big meetings and conferences, not to mention Sam's preaching services, were welcoming crowds. Every kind of man, woman, or child who wanted to have a part could come and freely participate. At the other end of the pendulum, as in the early ministry of Jesus Christ, dozens of individuals were making appointments and talking to members of the staff and others two by two. "Personal counseling," as it came to be called, was widespread. As with Nicodemus, the woman at the well, the rich young ruler, and innumerable others whom Jesus saw privately, so, in Calvary House and at luncheons and in other ways, individuals with problems were finding opportunities to discuss their needs privately with experienced Christians who had an answer.

But we had our "core" groups, as they might be called, at the center, the Peters and Jameses and Johns. On the staff and behind every meeting stood those who, by experience and conviction, were ultimately responsible. This was Jesus' way and we knew we couldn't improve upon it.

Let me illustrate by describing what happened in the Monday men's meeting. As this grew in numbers, a few who were concerned about its direction and quality found that they could come together an hour earlier to talk over plans for the larger meetings. We soon saw that the open group should be an opportunity to meet with God rather than just an occasion to talk about Him. If we had found a new life in Christ, this was what we must nurture and learn to give away. This took precedence over merely aiming for a good meeting. We should be ourselves. We should say honestly how we were making out in our personal lives, how we were carrying on our own quiet times, and when we had last talked convincingly about faith with another individual. Personal growth, life-changing, becoming redemptive in every situation—these should form the content of the larger group meetings. And we were to elicit participation, not use up the time talking too much ourselves. So we reviewed the possibilities, perhaps taking more time in such self-preparation for the open circle than we took at the more public session.

The results, as will be described in a later chapter, were exciting. Full participation resulted. There were pauses, moments of silence, but about these we did not worry; in fact, we welcomed them, for often the silence would be broken by a question or a statement from someone who had not previously spoken. And the resulting humor and give-and-take which occupied the next few minutes gave evidence of "the breeze of the Spirit."

The inner circle would always welcome a recruit who meant business, but it functioned like a heartbeat with its life-giving thrust. Those who felt a part of it became disciplined about their attendance and each was open and ready for whatever God seemed to indicate as his responsibility. And a desire grew, not merely to welcome newcomers at the open group but to follow up with individual men as one felt guided, and to make sure that each inquirer's needs were being met in every possible way and, wherever possible, answered.

* * *

It may not be everyone's destiny to become part of a small, life-giving team. Such great evangelists as Billy Graham and Corrie ten Boom, Gert Behanna and Norman Vincent Peale have their special programs and organizations. But in the grass roots, the few who commit themselves to one another as well as to God become the leaven, as Christ called them, in church, home, office, and community. Such commitment, with its openness to one another and the constant challenge to take a back seat in preferring one another, has always proved to be the hardest single factor in Christian discipleship. Fundamentally I am a lone wolf; temperamentally I want my own way; spiritually I am impatient and either feel inferior in my relationship with others or quite convinced that I see best and know the way it should be. To pool resources as well as possibilities requires a self-denial which I simply can't manufacture on my own. It has to be given to me, and to receive it I must take my hands off my own life and be ready and willing to follow not only where God leads but where my teammates lead.

Like several who have refused me their teamwork because, as they say, it is just too hard, my own reaction on many occasions is the same: "Father, this is just too hard."

But there stands Jesus, enlisting and working with a few fishermen. There He stands, deserted by lukewarm friends and criticized by the good people of His day. He traveled the roads with a few fellow workers and spent nights in the open with those who were willing to work with Him. Who am I to try to follow a less costly way? Yes, it may be "too hard" to live the open life which He lived Himself. But for me, hard or easy, it is the way that works, the way of the Cross, but also the way which inevitably, surprisingly, blossoms with "the breeze of the Spirit."

7/

A.A.'s Bill Wilson

*W*hen asked who he was, Bill would sometimes say, "Oh, just another guy who's one drink away from the gutter." The truth about alcoholics, as he came to see it, was just as simple as that. In his Gramercy Park days, long before he and "Doctor Bob" were sweating out their famous Twelve Steps in Akron, Ohio, the sobriety which Bill found, and maintained for the remaining thirty years of his life, had a kind of New Testament directness as its very cornerstone.

As a boy in Vermont, a slight tendency to gawkiness and stabs of inferiority prodded him into teen-age success. He early developed a fierce determination to win, and before leaving school he had become captain of his high-school baseball team as well as leader of the school's orchestra. For three years he studied engineering, then enlisted in the 66th Coast Artillery soon after America entered World War I. He went to France among the select, as a second lieutenant from the army's Plattsburgh (N.Y.) training camp, but not before discovering the liberating effects of a little social drinking. On his return he gravitated to Wall Street with what he refers to as a rather high opinion of himself. With little hesitation or direction, he plunged into various activities connected with the world of high finance. He took a law course at night and for awhile worked as an investigator for a surety company. On a motorcycle, with his wife Lois in a blue side car, he toured the Northeast, making confidential reports on the status of various small business enterprises. The drive for success was on.

Inevitably, Bill became involved in the stock market itself; business and financial leaders were his heroes. For several years Wall Street brought him money and applause. He and his charming Lois made an ever-widening circle of friends, and their style of living left nothing to be desired—superficially, that is. But all along, drinking was assuming a more important place, soon continuing all day and frequently most of the night. His friends and his young wife remonstrated. But many around him were getting rich, so "why not I?" thought Bill, liquor and all.

Then abruptly in October, 1929, all hell broke loose on the New York Stock Exchange, and the effect on Bill proved catastrophic. Here's the picture as he used to tell it at Gramercy Park:

After a seething day he would wobble from brokerage office to hotel bar and back again and find the ticker tape still clattering tardily about eight. Grabbing a strip, he would stare at an inch which read ABC-19. It might have been 54 that morning. Like most of his friends, he was soon finished. The evening papers were reporting more than one instance of a Wall Street leader hurling himself to death from some "tower of high finance," but such cowardice disgusted Bill. Tomorrow was another day. When drinking again at a bar, the old fierce determination to win always came back with overwhelming force.

One morning he 'phoned a friend in Montreal. Apparently there was still plenty of money in Canada, and by the following spring Lois and he were living north of the border and again in their accustomed style.

For awhile Bill felt like Napoleon freed from Elba, but not for long. On his travels his drinking problem stuck right with him. One generous friend after another had to let him go, and quite soon the Wilsons were again living in Brooklyn and broke. This time they stayed broke.

They found sanctuary with Lois's parents and she took a job as a salesgirl in a Manhattan department store, often reaching home exhausted to find Bill dead drunk. As for Bill, he had become an unwilling hanger-on in brokerage offices. He also loitered more and more at home where the liquor, which from a luxury had turned into a necessity, cost less. Remorse, hopelessness, even horror marked the next several years. His old courage to do battle had evaporated. Eating little or nothing when drinking, Bill was soon forty pounds underweight.

One short respite came after a visit to a nationally known New

York hospital for the rehabilitation of alcoholics. He had been sent there through the interest of his brother-in-law, a physician. A kind doctor, William D. Silkworth, who became his lifelong friend, not only explained how seriously ill he was but how (and why) his will power had become incapable of combating liquor. Bill felt that this partially excused his incredible behavior, so he returned to the Street and was soon making a little money again. But self-knowledge alone failed miserably to answer his problems, and the awful days of the drinking bouts returned all too soon. His family saw the undertaker or an asylum ahead, and Bill's loneliness turned into despair.

Meanwhile, on Gramercy Park, along with much personal work or personal counseling, various forces, including Sam Shoemaker's keen interest in programs for laymen, had encouraged the formation of midweek men's meetings characteristic of "A First Century Christian Fellowship," or "The Oxford Group," as this movement was now being called. In many of these weekly groups Christ's promise to His followers, that where two or three of them might gather in His name, He would personally be present, was being fulfilled. The meetings were lively and spiritually effective. The one held late in the afternoon every Thursday used an attractive, conveniently located lounge on the second floor of "61" and was presided over by an experienced member of the Calvary staff, or a leader in the wider fellowship, who knew the kind of questions businessmen and wage earners needed to air and discuss: answers to pressure, personal hang-ups, honesty in competitive business dealings, fear, or unemployment.

In God's own time and through a friend's rather casual visit to this group, the first gleam of hope was relayed to Bill. One bleak November afternoon Bill's phone rang. His old boarding-school friend and drinking companion, Ebby Thatcher, was on the other end of the wire. What surprised Bill was not so much that Ebby was in town but that he was sober, and when he arrived at the family residence in Brooklyn, he seemed strangely different from the hopeless man Bill had known. On the kitchen table stood a crock of pineapple juice and gin. Bill filled a glass and pushed it across as they sat down opposite each other. But smilingly Ebby refused.

Bill wondered what it was all about, but not for long. "I've got religion," volunteered Ebby without the slightest inhibition.

"Oh, not that!" Bill gulped a double mouthful of his brew. Then he sat glumly thinking there was nothing he could do but let his friend rant. Instead, Ebby related a short, moving story about two friends who, interceding in his favor several months before, had persuaded a New England judge to suspend sentence on a conviction in a case resulting from a brawl. They had professed faith in him, came up with a specific program of action—and it had worked.

Bill pretended to be unimpressed, but the story and especially Ebby's smile spoke to him eloquently. After all, he had always claimed to believe in a Power greater than himself. "What do you call this brand of religion?" he heard himself asking.

Ebby pretended to be tantalizingly vague. He mentioned an old church down on Gramercy Park and the friendliness shown him by men who met there week by week. "They're a great crowd," he added, "with some fresh ideas. They admit alcohol has 'em licked, so why shouldn't I? As one of them put it, 'Love's blind but the neighbors ain't!' When I took stock of myself the result was awful; but when I spilled the beans, confidentially, to another souse I felt like a new man. I also got some helpful thoughts about making a bit of what they call 'restitution.' I was told that there was no price tag on giving—if it's just giving yourself. And again it worked."

This time Bill, his long legs stretched out across the kitchen floor, was silent.

Ebby didn't stay long and he had no clincher, but he spoke quite seriously about a new experiment in prayer with which he was now starting every day. "Free as the air, too, Bill," he said, "because you only have to pray to God *as you think He is.*"

What could be fairer than that? Bill got the distinct impression that his friend was no longer fighting a drinking problem. No, the desire to imbibe had somehow just been lifted and he was asking daily for the power, not to struggle against alcohol but to live a life. Obviously he was finding it.

For several days Bill continued to mix his gin and fruit juice but he simply couldn't forget Ebby, not for a single waking moment. He felt rocked and stunned, but rather happily so. Ebby had not talked down to him nor given much advice. He felt the closeness of the old days in a fresh way. As he put it later, here was the kinship of common suffering and the enormously powerful influence of the simple fact of *one alcoholic talking to another.*

Viewed in the golden retrospect of the years to come this amounted to "round one" in Bill's fight for freedom.

* * *

In making him rector, Calvary Church had put several unexpected assets into Sam Shoemaker's hands, and none that he was to value more than a mission for down-and-outs on East Twenty-third Street. Connected with it was a rooming house called The Olive Tree Inn. Presided over by Harry Hadley and "Tex" Francisco, Calvary Mission provided evening meetings and simple meals, a place to sleep, and, for those who were finding freedom from liquor, a warm fellowship for hopeless men. Since he totally lacked resources, Ebby had gone there to live. With the men he met, and with the new friends in nearby Gramercy Park, he now enjoyed an ever-increasing number of close relationships.

Bill knew where Ebby was and one day, between his mood swings and while still "pretty maudlin," he got the bright idea of doing a bit of religious investigation by paying Ebby a call. Unfortunately, it was a long walk from the nearest subway station to Calvary Mission and Bill began stopping in bars as he traveled east on Twenty-third Street. Most of the afternoon slipped by between drinks and he was in high fettle in a drunken way by the time he finally reached the mission's front door. He had picked up a Finnish sailmaker and this unruly pair were on the point of being refused admission when Ebby himself appeared, quickly appraised the situation, and suggested a plate of beans. After the food had been washed down with copious cups of black coffee, the newcomers heard there would shortly be a meeting in the mission hall. Would they like to go? Certainly, they said, that was why they were there.

Sitting on one of the hard wooden pews that filled the hall, Bill shivered at the sight of the derelict audience. There followed a few hymns and prayers and then an exhortation by Tex, the evening's leader. Only Jesus could save, he said, and strangely enough his words failed to jar. Whatever he meant, Bill felt he must be right. He listened with rising excitement as certain men got up and gave testimonials. Then came "the call." As various men started forward, Bill found himself, unaccountably motivated, heading for the altar. Ebby grabbed for his coattails but it was too late. He knelt, shaking the more, among the penitents and felt, perhaps for the first time, truly penitent himself. He had a wild impulse to talk and this he did with deep earnestness and in a way that compelled attention.

Afterwards, sitting in the dormitory in the building next door, where Ebby was living, he could remember scarcely a word he had said. Ebby, obviously relieved, told him he had done all right and had "given his life to God."

This experience may be called "round two."

When he reached home Bill gave a full account of his experience to Lois, and they had a long and earnest talk. It seemed significant to both of them that on his return trip along Twenty-third Street he had never once thought of going into a bar. This was something very new!

Came the dawn, and Bill realized that he had slept like a baby and without an ounce of gin. He had only a slight hangover, not the devastating head he had expected. But his old habits still gripped him. He would not be a fanatic about this new life. He would take another drink or two just by way of tapering off.

When Lois had left for work, the process became easier, and instead of tapering off he took a couple more and nicely succeeded in tapering *on*. At six o'clock his wife found him upstairs on the bed and, of course, drunk.

So it went for two grim days; but Ebby's smile and the mission experience never left him. On the morning of the third day his wandering thoughts gathered into a sharp focus as he began to compare himself to a victim of cancer. Surely if he had cancer he would not sit at home and put cold cream on the affected parts. Certainly not! He would look up the best doctor in the business and put himself unreservedly into his hands. So now he would return to the hospital and his old friend Dr. Silkworth. Here at least he would be helped to sober up, and then perhaps he could take a fresh look at Ebby's formula for sobriety.

He arrived at the hospital in wretched shape, having consumed two bottles of beer en route. According to all accounts, Dr. Silkworth met him in the hall. In very high spirits Bill waved a third bottle in the doctor's face, and yelled, "At last, Doc, I've found something!" At this the good doctor's face fell, and Bill realized all the more how deeply the medical man loved him. The doctor merely shook his head and intimated that it might be time for Bill to get upstairs and into bed.

Some three days passed. The effects of both the alcohol and the sedatives he had been given wore off. In their place Bill suffered a dull sense of emptiness and depression. As he put it, he was "still choking on the God business." Then, bright and early one morning he saw Ebby's smiling face before him again, Ebby in person. Ah, thought Bill, here's where he thinks he's going to evangelize me. He waited suspiciously but nothing happened except that Ebby entered the room and sat down.

Finally it was Bill who spoke. "What's that neat little formula once more?" he asked. In perfect good humor Ebby recited the group precepts again. You admit you are licked. You get honest with yourself. You talk things out with somebody else. If possible you make restitution to the people you have harmed. You try to give of yourself without stint and with no demand for reward. And you pray to whatever God you think there is, entirely as an experiment. It was as simple and as mysterious as that.

After some small talk, Ebby again vanished. Bill's depression deepened unbearably. It seemed to him as though he were now at the very bottom of the pit. He still gagged badly on the notion of approaching that "Power greater than yourself," but the last vestige of his pride and obstinacy had been crushed.

Then quite suddenly he found himself crying out, "If there is a God, let Him show Himself. I am ready to do anything, *anything!*"

At this the whole room lit up with a great light reminiscent of the Spirit of Christmas Present in Dicken's *A Christmas Carol*. Bill could only describe it by saying that he had been caught up in an ecstasy. In his mind's eye he saw himself on the top of a high mountain with the wind of the Spirit blowing. The acute sense that burst upon him that he was a free man was crucial.

This proved to be his third and in a sense his final "round."

Slowly his ecstasy subsided, and instead he felt a great peace and a presence which he could only identify as the supernatural Presence of the Living God. No matter how terrible the past had been, of one thing he was sure—the future was to be all right for it was to be with Him.

When Dr. Silkworth next stopped in, Bill tried to give him an account of his astonishing experience. He feared the doctor might feel that he was hallucinating or losing his mind. But the reverse proved to be the doctor's attitude. He immediately encouraged

Bill to hold on to the reality of all he had gone through. "You're by no means going crazy," he said. "Some basic psychological or spiritual event has happened. Hang on to it. *Anything* is better than the way you were."

Then faithful Ebby called again, this time with a worn copy of *Varieties of Religious Experience* by the great Harvard psychologist, William James. Together they devoured parts of it. Spiritual experiences, James had written, were gifts from the blue but they could transform people. Often they were preceded by pain, suffering, or calamity. Complete hopelessness and "deflation at depth" were almost always part of the picture. Bill took it all personally, for this was his own history, especially the realization that deflation at depth had ushered in the spiritual renewal and freedom he now felt.

Before the day was out he was already focused on changing the world, and when he was dismissed from the hospital, he started out after drunks like a person on jet propulsion. He envisioned a chain reaction that would dry up the nation. But actually his next necessary lesson was the old adage that patience is a virtue.

As part of the new life, he threw himself into group activity both at Calvary House and Calvary Mission. He took on alcoholics by the score; some would clear up for a little while but then flop dismally. Bill maintained his own sobriety, however, but at the end of six months nobody else had become sober for long. Unfortunately he wasn't meeting men at their own point of need, as Ebby had done for him. Instead he was trying to impose Robert E. Speer's four "absolute standards" from the Sermon on the Mount. These standards, that had often been used so wisely by Oxford Group leaders and others on people who were physically sick and mentally obsessed, were now backfiring.

Dr. Silkworth was one of the first to underline Bill's mistaken approach. "You're *preaching* at these fellows, Bill," he said, in essence, "although no one ever preached at you. Turn your strategy around. Remember Professor James's insistence that 'deflation at great depth' is the foundation of most spiritual experiences like your own. Give your new contacts the *medical* business—and hard. Describe the obsession that condemns men to drink and the physical sensitivity or allergy of the body that makes this type go mad or die if they keep on drinking."

Bill saw the point and heartily agreed. However, not a little pressure continued to be brought on him by some of his new friends who wanted him to forget his alcoholics and get on with "changing the world." For his part, Bill knew that he was being called to go for something more specific, and that more than anything else he wanted to work with alcoholics. In this Sam Shoemaker remained a staunch ally, for despite his immersion in both group and parish work, Sam well remembered his own signal failure with the few drunks to whom he had given rooms in Calvary House instead of at The Olive Tree Inn. Who could forget? One of these had gleefully tossed an alarm clock out of a fourth floor window in the dead of night, putting it neatly through a stained-glass window of the church. At early communion the next morning the clergy had suddenly noticed it on the embroidered cloth of the high altar. Sam realized further that the pull on Bill to work with others who were handicapped as he had been represented something very special. While he remained just as unclear as Bill as to where and how this "ministry" would finally take root, he strongly shared Bill's desire to explore his true vocation and look for an open door through which he might fulfill it.

* * *

Strangely enough Bill's chance came not in New York City but among another crowd of Oxford Group friends in Akron, Ohio. In looking for work Bill had drifted back to Wall Street again, still completely sober but very frustrated. One day, through a chance acquaintance in a brokerage office, he got himself mixed up in a proxy fight involving a small manufacturing company in the Midwest. He and a few others visited Ohio to look into things. Again in fine fettle, Bill could already see himself as the company's new president; but when the chips were down the other side had more proxies and Bill and his friends got ousted.

At this point everyone but Bill returned to New York. With no more than ten dollars in his pocket, he found himself at the Mayflower Hotel in Akron on the eve of Mother's Day—and alone. As he paced the hotel lobby he could see the bar filling up at one end and hear the familiar buzz of conversation mounting. But God was with him. He recalled clearly that it had always been *by trying to help other alcoholics* that he had stayed sober himself.

That was it, he thought. He must find another alcoholic to talk to. Down deep he realized for the first time that he needed that other alcoholic just as much as the man he wanted to help needed him.

Across from the bar at the far end of the lobby he paused by a church directory. Then quite at random he called an Episcopal priest and to his listener's amazement poured out his tale. Finally he asked if the minister knew of someone who could put him in touch with another alcoholic. When the good man realized what Bill was looking for, he may well have envisioned two people getting drunk instead of one. In any event he finally got Bill's point and came up with a list of some ten people who might be able to help.

Still in the 'phone booth Bill began calling. It was a Saturday afternoon and scarcely anyone was home. One line was busy and the few people who did answer failed to respond. Bill got down to the very last name, but this one call did the trick. A young married woman, Henrietta Seiberling, answered. She had no drinking problem herself, she said, but she knew a man, a doctor, who indeed did need help. She suggested that Bill come straight over and pursue things further.

So it was that within twenty-four hours Bill stood face to face with "Dr. Bob" who, with his wife, Anne, had gone to several group meetings in Akron, and who was later to become A.A. member number two and cofounder with Bill of Alcoholics Anonymous.

Nothing seemed very promising at the time. Dr. Bob and Anne came in. The doctor, visibly shaking, explained that he could only stay for a minute. However, their hostess discreetly led the two men to a small library and there they went on talking until after eleven o'clock. Bill kept reminding himself that previously, in New York, his aggressive approach had backfired, so he proceeded carefully, with no mention of the fireworks of his own full-blown religious experience. He bore down on an alcoholic's allergy to liquor and his obsession with drink once he got started. Though Dr. Bob was a medical doctor this was news to him, *bad* news. But here they were, two drunks, face to face, and one of them with an answer. This mutual give-and-take became the very heart of A.A. in the days to come. As Bill talked the doctor relaxed. "Yes, that's me," he began to say. "I'm like that." They were talking the same language.

As it worked out, Bill went to live with Dr. Bob and Anne. Every morning they experimented in having their devotions together. As Bill described it later, Anne would sit in the corner by the fireplace and read from the Bible, and then they would huddle together in the stillness awaiting inspiration and guidance. The final missing link in Bill's program had been located and new insights were given. Both men felt the immense importance of continuing to work with other alcoholics and, through contacts at the Akron City Hospital, the third and fourth members of A.A. were reached, helped, and included in their fellowship.

*   *   *

Besides that first Akron group, on Bill's return East, there soon developed a weekly meeting in the Wilson's Brooklyn parlor. When Bill visited Sam Shoemaker, who had been keenly following his progress, the two had a memorable reunion. After a few months, several meeting places opened up, such as a room in New York's Steinway Hall, one in a Manhattan tailoring shop, and others in suburban homes. Gradually groups began to appear in other cities—Philadelphia, Washington, Baltimore, and Cleveland. An A.A. ferment had begun to work and the good news began to spread rapidly. Today every city in the land and hundreds overseas—one might say almost every hamlet—has its A.A. group. And the end is never in sight. For alcoholism has become a major illness throughout the world, Praise God that, through the faithfulness and experience of two men, this growing problem has an answer—adequate, effective, and immediately at hand.

The Twelve Steps of Alcoholics Anonymous*

According to Lois Wilson, when Bill was writing the "big" A.A. book in 1938, he thought of his many talks with Dr. Bob about the importance of stressing the spiritual aspect of the program. He therefore expanded the original six steps, which they had learned from the Oxford Groups, into the famous Twelve Steps now used around the world. He had a deep desire to make it impossible for

---

* Reprinted with permission of A.A. World Services Inc., copyright owners, P.O. Box 459, Grand Central Station, N.Y., N.Y. 10017.

an alcoholic who wanted sobriety to find a single loophole. The steps have never since been altered.

Step One: We admitted that we were powerless over alcohol—that our lives had become unmanageable.

Step Two: Came to believe that a Power greater than ourselves could restore us to sanity.

Step Three: Made a decision to turn our will and our lives over to the care of God *as we understood Him.*

Step Four: Made a searching and fearless moral inventory of ourselves.

Step Five: Admitted to God, to ourselves, and to another human being the exact nature of our wrongs.

Step Six: Were entirely ready to have God remove all these defects of character.

Step Seven: Humbly asked Him to remove our shortcomings.

Step Eight: Made a list of all persons we had harmed, and became willing to make amends to them all.

Step Nine: Made direct amends to such people whenever possible, except when to do so would injure them or others.

Step Ten: Continued to take personal inventory and when we were wrong promptly admitted it.

Step Eleven: Sought through prayer and meditation to improve our conscious contact with God *as we understood Him,* praying only for knowledge of His will for us and the power to carry that out.

Step Twelve: Having had a spiritual awakening as the result of these steps, we tried to carry this message to alcoholics, and to practice these principles in all our affairs.

8 /
A Jewish Teacher
Discovers the Messiah

*I*n the early years of the Great Depression a Jewish high-school teacher in Brooklyn was brought into touch with Calvary House through a notice on the church page of *The New York Times.*

Like many intellectuals, he had found steady advancement in his classroom work and had become assistant principal of his school. But secretly he was a deeply frustrated man. Behind a front of pretense and self-sufficiency he constantly felt an anguished sense of inadequacy.

Bernie Gair's avocation was reading, especially all manner of philosophic and religious literature. One might say that his neighborhood tavern was the local bookstore—or any place where he could find secondhand books.

One day he carried home a faded blue hardback called *Life Changers* by the English writer, Harold Begbie. He didn't like the title, but the book quickly captivated him for it focused on a revolutionary experience of the Living God which eight young university men had recently encountered, four of them American and the other four British. One was a British army captain who had returned to Oxford from Flanders; another, called "Persona Grata" in the book, was Sherry Day, a graduate of Yale.

In reading and rereading this book, Bernie Gair suddenly realized that one of these very men, according to *The Times,* would be speaking at a public gathering at 61 Gramercy Park within a few days. This man was to be on a panel which would include businessmen and other New Yorkers. Bernie was intrigued and determined to go and see what it was all about.

The following Thursday found Gair seated in an inconspicuous seat at the back of the Great Hall at Calvary House. The speakers proved to be individuals with whom he could easily identify, and he felt sure that Sam Shoemaker, the chairman, was none other than the man described in the Begbie book as "the Virginian." The repeated illustrations of the personal nature of faith delighted him, as did the stories detailing the varied ways in which faith had "worked." But what surprised him most was a spontaneous hilarity which often broke out despite the deadly seriousness of the questions dealt with.

He rode the subway home in a daze, but he was elated by what he had heard and determined to find out more about the sponsors who, according to the newspaper notice, were known as A First Century Christian Fellowship. They had something, a quality of life with a serenity and a sense of purpose quite foreign to his own experience.

Three days later he attended a Sunday service at Calvary Church and met Sam Shoemaker who was busily greeting worshippers on the porch of the church.

"We've not met you before," Sam Shoemaker said, smiling.

"That's right," answered Bernie. "I'm a teacher from Brooklyn but I did come to your meeting last Thursday."

"Tell you what," said the minister. "Come back tomorrow afternoon about 5:30. We have a men's group in Calvary House and there we can get to talk."

Monday night at the appointed time Bernie Gair arrived. He sat down close to the door of the stairway from which he had entered, displaying both the caution and curiosity of most new visitors. Introducing himself, he carefully explained that, as an inquirer, he had just come to listen. But obviously what he heard that night he liked, for he reappeared week after week, always friendly and gracious but careful not to reveal his inner reactions. I think he knew from the start that he had found kindred spirits and that the day might come when he would have plenty to say. In an article printed several years later in *The Evangel,* he wrote: "I left that first group with a hunger to have the same inner freedom and sense of purpose I saw in the faces of those around me."

The rigorous training of a Jewish boy and an acquaintance with the Old Testament prophets and the Talmudic literature put Bernie in a prize position from which to evaluate religious meetings. He came to know dozens of men in the Monday fellowship, some of them intimately. And he often lingered afterwards, talking with people and comparing notes.

The old group had an aphorism: "Grass is green and crows are black the whole world over." Bernie Gair accepted this as a helpful hint about human nature and welcomed his repeated chances to reappraise his own behavioral standards. As he did so, the initial sense of dissatisfaction with himself deepened, and from this he never shrank. As he later said: "My newly acquired friends put no pressure on me to accept a single dogma about Jesus. They simply held him up as 'the way' and invited me to consider traveling in it. . . . A person can learn a lot by measuring his life against the straight edges of Moses' moral law, as summarized in Jesus' absolute principles. I began to see my shabbiness, mediocrities, meanness, and dishonesties, and a new word came alive in my vocabulary: *sin*. It was not a word held in high repute in my circles, or even considered in good taste. People made mistakes, failed to achieve, suffered from complexes, had faults. But sin? No."

Bernie's new friends continued to challenge him indirectly with questions put in various ways. Was a man willing to make an honest assessment of his life in the light of God's standards as seen in Jesus? Would an inquirer be willing to yield to God the governance of his life, and attempt to live henceforth according to His will through the power of His Spirit? This would mean a compact with God. Later, Bernie wrote: "I realized that I would have to abdicate sovereignty of myself and my affairs and believe that God would daily guide me, forgive me, strengthen me, and feed me from a new center. My final question was how was I to *know* for certain that I was building on spiritual bedrock, and not on escapism or wish fulfillment?"

As the teacher wrestled with these questions, he saw a bright side. He came to realize that Christian faith need not negate the teachings of the Hebrew Law and the Prophets. All *that* had been like a training ground for the spirit, a revelation of man's need for a redeemer. Bernie asked himself: "Had He come?" He began to see that Jesus, though an obscure resident of a small town, a mere carpenter, was perhaps the one who had been previsioned by the Old Testament sages and described in their Scriptures as God's special agent—"the spotless lamb of the temple," the Messiah, the Savior, the Christ, the Son of God.

Then there came a special day. With a new clarity about God and about himself, Bernie Gair felt compelled to act.

"I made a decision," he said. "Quietly, in my own room, I prayed God to take over. I yielded my life to Him in a step of self-commitment and, believe me, *something happened.* I experienced a tremendous sense of release; fresh power had been born within me."

Bernie shared his experience with the Monday group and there was great rejoicing. But happy as he was, he believed that something further still needed to be done, that his private experience now required an act of a public nature.

Sam Shoemaker felt this, too. One Sunday soon thereafter, though unaware of the step the Brooklyn teacher had taken privately, he stopped Bernie on the porch of the church and asked the simple question, "When is it going to take place?" Both men understood each other.

The next afternoon Bernie once again seemed strangely silent, but when the Monday group broke up he drew the convener aside and asked, "Is there any reason why I shouldn't be baptized?" To the older man the situation seemed like a scene from the Book of Acts. "Any reason against it? I should say not. It would be wonderfully good."

"Yes, it would be good," said Bernie. "But I'd rather not have the baptism part of a large service. My wife is not in sympathy. Why don't you and just one other man from the group stand with me, and of course the rector, say next Monday, an hour before our regular meeting?" And so it happened and Bernie publicly stepped into the new way of life.

This decision to follow Christ did not stop here. One of Bernie's keenest desires was to reach other Jewish people and help them to make "the great discovery" too. To this end he allied himself with Jewish Christians whom he located not only in Manhattan but in Chicago and Baltimore. One highly respected group published a quarterly called *The Interpreter* to which Bernie became a frequent contributor. Today he is the magazine's associate editor. In everything he seems to say: "Wait a moment. Reexamine the evidence. In Jesus Christ, the Messiah has already come!"

In the privacy of his home, Bernie staked out regular, unhurried times when he could "feed" on the Scriptures, meditate, and "listen" to God. He admitted that he often found it necessary to bring before God a recurrence of his stubbornness of heart, outcroppings of pride, or discouragement at not always being able to keep order in his classrooms. Joyfully, he kept reminding more conventional believers of the power of forgiveness through the simple act of recommitment.

In the public school where he taught, despite the general disinclination of his fellow teachers to mention religion, Bernie began to invite a few of his teen-age boys to meet with him for an hour after classes. With a nucleus of eight, four black students and four white, he formed a group known as the Trinity Club. One rather hard-boiled pupil, a declared agnostic, heard about these activities through his girl friend. He began reading the Bible on his own. He found, to his surprise, that it "made sense," and he asked if he could join in.

Bob was far less inhibited than Bernie had been, and before long he told the club that he had some good news: he had decided to let God run his life. At one of the meetings he summed up how things were working out: "I still sin plenty of times. As you might say, the flesh is corrupt but my soul is new and no longer gives in to my natural desires. There's often a battle raging inside me, but now when I am tempted, I call upon the Holy Spirit for help. This may not be forthcoming in the way I want it . . . but what I get is much better than what I asked for. My loneliness is gone . . . everyday is a new experience . . . and what I now want more than anything else is to let other guys know about God and see them find the same exit from the maze."

As for Bernie, let no one suppose that his new experience led to unbroken happiness and unmitigated success. His faith in the discovery of his Messiah was costly. Because he had become a Christian, the principal of a Jewish parochial school in which he gave a course told him politely but bluntly that his services would "no longer be required."

"So you see," Bernie said softly one Monday at the group meeting, "I've lost my second-string job. . . . And I don't know what to do. That work meant everything, especially to my wife and the boys. We were counting on the extra income to send them to college."

Several in the group that day had lost jobs in a similarly abrupt fashion. They told how they felt about their losses, their anxieties, and their fears. As Bernie listened, we could see him relax. He realized he was not alone but had a close relationship with everyone in the room. He was aware of a renewed oneness with God.

9/
Creating a Christian Cell

*W*hen the Oxford Group had become Moral Re-Armament, their leadership moved away from Calvary House and an interruption took place in the laymen's work of the parish. Most group meetings stopped for a while. The editorship of *The Calvary Evangel*, later *Faith at Work*, came into my hands and, soon afterwards, many of those closest to Sam Shoemaker and active in our broader fellowship gathered at "61" to appraise the situation and clarify our goals and purposes.

Not without good reason had Frank Buchman come to the conclusion that the church's view of evangelism was out-of-date and the pace of its outreach too slow. Yet to many Calvary parishioners and to most readers of *The Evangel* the church represented the primary focal point where the spiritual fire so urgently needed in our country could and should be rekindled. And it was through the church's facilities that we wished to work in serving, variously, to extend the Kingdom of God throughout our nation and in every possible place around the world.

Many other factors and a conflict of personalities further confused the Calvary picture, which in the mid-thirties was without doubt a somewhat tragic one. But such a vast amount of experience had been acquired through the old group and so many valuable lessons had been learned by the "Calvary family" that, notwithstanding the confusion and the hurt, there prevailed a strong sense of gratitude to the leaders of all that had been initiated, so modestly at first, under the name of A First Century Christian Fellowship.

Those of us who chose to continue to work within the church found that we shared a wealth of conviction about the primary principles of this ancient establishment and the reality and availability of the Holy Spirit. Most of those making up this ongoing core also continued to realize the urgent need for people everywhere to understand the nature and prevalence of evil and the necessity for personal forgiveness for sin. As we corresponded with one another, we sensed our opportunity to bring hope and, under God, new life to those with whom we were in touch. The main need was a simple willingness for people to be honest about themselves and loving toward other people. These were, of course, long-established group principles. In fact, the norm continued to be a zealous quest for the kind of faith men would be able to pass on constantly to others in home, office, and local communities.

The *Evangel* went straight ahead publishing more and more stories of "a faith that works," stories that came from the daily lives of ordinary people who, in the Spirit, were accomplishing extraordinary feats in abundant living and in healing. These stories and Sam Shoemaker's own succession of new books circulated ever more widely, until we found that kindred spirits were corresponding with us at "61" from every state in the union and a large number of countries overseas.

The reappearance of weekly group meetings at Calvary took place shortly through a dramatic personal experience which, in turn, was motivated by the continuing spirit of fellowship at "61." Secretly thrilled by the chance I now had to develop work similar to that which I had carried on earlier at the Princeton University Press, I found the editing of a 32- or 48-page monthly journal enormously interesting. With spontaneous enthusiasm, I poured myself into this, and into the writing of such items as editorials and Bible studies—and *The Evangel* flourished. However, after a while the rapid pace took its toll. Certainly I neglected my family disgracefully. I realized that the pressure of deadlines and re-writes was weighing on me most uncomfortably, and at the same time I found that my imagination was becoming tinged with unhealthy impressions and impure thoughts. I was "out of conceit with myself," as the English author, Herbert Gray, once put it.

Knowing that the sooner this troublesome state of mind was mended the better, I determined to see and talk with the rector as well as with my wife. The latter usually "knew all about it"; but to be honest with the man for whom I worked, and in a way which would "pour contempt on all my pride," represented a step with a higher price tag. Previously, such openness had let in the breeze of the Spirit, and I knew it would do so again.

But alas, the morning when I asked at the Calvary switchboard for Sam Shoemaker, I was chagrined at being told that he was out, or couldn't be disturbed—I don't remember which. The urgency in my heart sent me looking for a substitute father confessor. I roved about the building and even visited offices in the basement without results. Then, as I was about to abandon my plan, I unexpectedly ran straight into Herbert Lantau, our 250-pound building engineer, a person whom I knew only slightly.

Herbie, a great hulk of a man, saw me at once and cheerily called out, "Morning, Irv. What's on your mind?"

"Oh, nothing much," I said. But then in a burst of honesty, I reversed myself and blurted out, "Actually *plenty*. A whole mass of personal conflicts with which I need help. Maybe we could have a talk."

"You bet," said Herbie, all too heartily. "Fire away."

"Not here. Not on your life!" I answered. "Perhaps around back where we can close the door. But not in this semipublic place where our voices may even reach the lobby."

And so it happened. We filed back and around the basement, a hundred feet or so, where we switched on the lights of an inside, stuffy enclosure known as the choir robing room and stood gazing at each other, rather embarrassed, neither of us knowing quite what was coming next. But I realized I'd asked for it.

"Herbie," I said, "I'm just a mess—a complete hypocrite. Here I am writing all these highfalutin' editorials and my mind's like a sink. This city, with its nightclubs and countless neon signs of naked females, has my imagination roaring. Besides, the pressure of work alone, with so many demands and not enough time, is driving me crazy. I've talked it over with my wife, but I believe that letting a fellow like you know the score will give my pride a deeper blow. Then perhaps I can tell the Lord what a stinker I am and ask His forgiveness."

Herbie looked astonished. "O.K., O.K.," he said. "But take it easy." We sat down and I continued. When I had finished he smiled most lovingly. "I'll pray with you, Irv. But first you must give me a chance to say a few things about myself. I believe I can more than match every single thing you've said by something quite similar in my own life. Now you listen to *me* for a minute." And with that he put some of his own sins on the mat.

Then, like a couple of kids at bedtime, we slipped to our knees with no notice of the hard cement floor. Rather emotionally I expressed to God the sorrow I felt at finding myself still such an unsavory person, and Herbie immediately followed me with an equally honest admission of failure and need.

What a relief! What unexpected liberation! It's never easy to put into words this central Christian experience of forgiveness which comes like a breeze, not through remorse but with true repentance. Suddenly one feels so palpably freed from depressing evil, and so restored and refreshed with renewed hope. Paradoxical? I suppose it is. Further, one realizes the whole experience is directly if strangely related to the life and work of Jesus Christ. As a Christian, I saw again that *He* has been the gateway. The old was gone and not at all as a result of merit or self-effort. At the very same moment, the sweetness and the possibilities of the future broke vividly upon me once again.

We remained kneeling for a moment. Then standing there, along with a deep sense of gratitude, we both had the same desire to let some of our friends in on this privilege we had experienced of the reality and availability of God's love.

"When could you be available if we should ask fellows like Tom and Des and a few others to join us?" I asked Herbert.

"Oh, almost any day about five or so."

"Right. Then why don't we each mention such a possibility to the few men in the parish we know best. And how about this coming Monday afternoon, say on the second floor?"

"Swell!" said Herbie.

Quickly we listed and divided up a dozen names, and then without more ado slapped each other on the back and parted, the sexton to return to his office and I, whistling, to my editorial quarters on the fourth floor. A burden had simply rolled off our backs, and, when we later contacted our friends, we didn't need any detailed explanation to back up our suggestions.

"Whatcha goin' to do?" some of them asked. We said we didn't quite know but that we were not just holding another meeting. We wanted to tell about our recent experience and have a chance for informal fellowship, a time when different ones could say pretty much anything that was on their minds, and perhaps see some next steps in God's plan for their lives.

Then, with but one or two exceptions, our friends came, and from the start "Monday at five-thirty" became a lively time and most of us began to look forward eagerly to it. In fact, this new group carried on for years, new faces continually appearing. When the meetings grew too big, the group simply spawned other groups like the one described in Chapter 11 which Ralston Young, "Red Cap 42," began at Grand Central Terminal.

As our parent group grew, we also arranged for a preliminary session an hour earlier. Four or five of those whom God was using most consistently (at any given period) would come to an upstairs office and have a chance to talk and pray unhurriedly before the later meeting began. How important this became for training in leadership is revealed in the story about Bernie Gair in the preceding chapter. At the larger group we then strove to meet *with* God and not just let the friends present talk *about* Him. We always broke up well before seven. Sometimes we then adjourned for a dinner group and we also often made appointments for follow-up with men who wished to talk privately.

No one was ever required to make conversation, only to give his name and tell how he happened to be with us. The aims were three: (1) to find a more living personal faith; (2) to learn how to pass this on to others; and (3) to see how to apply faith, practically, in our homes and offices—in fact, in all the situations in which we found ourselves.

As examples of what took place almost immediately among those who first attended these meetings, consider the changes in the lives of a salesman and an architect. The former, Tom Page, had served in the United States Navy in World War I. When we came to know him, he was still bending his elbow far too frequently. The architect, Desmond Upton, had made blueprints for many New York buildings, the Ritz-Carlton being one of them, but he had become a confirmed alcoholic. Long before the flowering of A.A., he had discovered an extraordinary and instantaneous liberation from the compulsive use of liquor through a wise, older layman whom Sam Shoemaker had on his staff for a time as a volunteer.

One Monday, Tom smilingly affirmed, "Ah just try to be redemptive in every sale ah make. [He talked with a delightful Southern drawl.] And it's amazin' how many people seem to be just waitin' to talk about religion."

DES: "Of course you've got a lot of faith yourself, as I have, to start with."

TOM: "Yeah, but ah remember to give myself again to Christ every time ah start makin' sales calls."

DES (thoughtfully): "You mean you're not satisfied just to be sober and right-minded yourself? You're out to get others? I call that buttonholing! I don't like it."

TOM (still smiling): "No? Well, there's no buttonholin' about it. Ah just tell other folks what Jesus Christ has done for me and some of them want what I've found for themselves. Then we forget sales talk and perhaps have some prayer."

DES (very red in the face and turning to the moderator): "Well, I know how wonderfully God has freed me from liquor. I walked straight through the Commodore bar the other night on the way to the train and just waved pleasantly to my friends who were at the rail. But I've never considered taking my faith as seriously as Tom here and trying to get someone else to accept what I believe."

MODERATOR: "No, Des, but you *could.*"

DES: "Now wait a minute! This is all brand new. Don't push me."

At this remark everyone laughed, and the talk moved around the circle. But when the meeting broke up, the chairman of the day sidled over to Des and asked him if he'd like to talk a bit more about what Tom had said. Yes, he would. So the two men skipped supper and moved into an adjoining room and continued to consider what Jesus had meant by "fishing for men."

After all, the moderator affirmed, one of the very first things our Lord said to the young men who first joined Him in His work was that if they went along with Him, He would teach them how to become "fishers of men."

"Yes, I see that now," said the other. "It's a brand new idea to me. I'd have to make a whole new surrender of myself to God and I don't believe I'm ready. Anyway, I'd fall straight on my face in this 'fishing' business. I'd just make too many mistakes."

"Ah, but that's all part of what you'd trust God with. He'll take care of your mistakes. The quality of life with Him at the center means a childlike trust. You will doubtless pull some boners, but you need have no fear. This whole group is still a fellowship of sinners."

And again the talk continued until suddenly Des, with a face even redder than before, said, "All right. Let's get it over with." Dropping to his knees by a long couch, and with the other man by his side, he told God he was ready to let go of himself—his fears as well as everything else—and take the harder road of becoming a vocal Christian, the road his friend Tom was traveling. Both the moderator and he renewed their commitments to God, and then, as they stood up, the tears simply streamed down Des's cheeks. He was laughing as he brushed them off and he slapped the shoulder of his companion. "Thanks, thanks, so much," he said. "I'm going to run for a late train, but things are going to be different." And indeed they were. Not only did the architect become vocal, and quite effectively so, but a new relationship was born in his family life and we found out later that his wife, Florence, had also become "one of us."

As for Tom, he and his wife Blanche never missed a chance to speak the word of faith. (Blanche had an antique shop on Madison Avenue.) In fact it was Tom who first caught the imagination of "Gert" Behanna, once a confirmed socialite who had reached the point where, as she put it herself, she depended on benzedrine to get her up in the morning, gin to keep her going, and phenobarbitol to knock her out at night.

Sitting next to her at a dinner party in New Canaan, Connecticut, Tom listened to her startling list of malpractices, which included plenty of drugs on top of liquor. Then he smiled and asked, "Why don't you just turn the whole lot over to God?"

Gert was furious. But she followed Tom into the living room after dinner and allowed as how it made her sick to hear anyone talk as if a person could just toss all one's troubles to God like handing a suitcase to a redcap. Tom, still smiling, assured her, yes, that was just what he meant.

A week later, back in Chicago, Gert did just that in the privacy of her own study with the result that she became a brand new person and, in turn, a spectacularly successful spokeswoman for the Lord God Almighty in her own right.

10 /

A Magazine
for a Worldwide Family

The single most exhilarating activity in which I engaged during my years with Sam Shoemaker concerned *The Calvary Evangel*, the monthly parish publication which, first as *The Evangel* and then as *Faith at Work*, became known in over a hundred countries around the world. This magazine had started with nothing but the good intentions and enthusiasm of a few members of an ancient Calvary Church Men's Association. Its subscription income covered about half of its total costs. Yet it grew and frequently flourished, like the green bay tree. The secret was quite simple: it carried the personal stories of ordinary people who, through faith, were living in an extraordinary way. Like the parables of our Lord, the stories literally gave Christian faith away. Readers wanted them, *had* to have them, whether they paid the regular price, got the magazine free, or, in not a few instances, contributed more than the subscription rate in order to keep the magazine alive and expanding.

Volume 1, Copy 1 appeared back in 1888 when a few vigorous laymen petitioned their rector, Dr. Satterlee, for permission to publish a journal which would carry the living truths of his sermons to a wider audience than the regular occupants of the church pews. They wanted the news they heard on Sunday mornings to reach the shut-ins and the ill, and also as many others as possible beyond the confines of the parish.

On the first masthead, the imaginative founders of the new journal forthrightly proclaimed:

"The initial number of our Parish Paper makes its appearance at the opening of the Advent Season, and being as its name implies, 'a Herald of Good Tidings' . . . it has been suggested that the paper should have as its motto 'Thy Kingdom Come.' The very nature of the contents of the paper will, we hope, suggest no other thought."

What a way to begin! And how heartened would those now long-departed editors be could they but picture the history of their publication and the response it continues to receive from Christians and non-Christians alike almost a hundred years later!

A notable aspect of Sam Shoemaker's ministry at Calvary Church was his continuing use of the printed word, including *The Calvary Evangel*. He had been rector for less than two years when he first appeared in print as an author with *"A Young Man's View of the Ministry* (Association Press, 1923), eloquently proclaiming the merits of the ministry as a vocation; and with *Realizing Religion* (Association Press, 1921), giving, in a wider way, the validity—nay the necessity—of Christian faith for the average American. At the same time he printed in each issue of the parish magazine both a current sermon and the story of an individual whose life had recently been revolutionized by God through contact with him and others on the Calvary staff. His books quite rapidly went overseas, especially to people being touched by his friends in the Oxford Group, and articles by him soon came out in a variety of American religious journals.

All this had a beneficial effect on the circulation of *The Evangel* itself, as many who read his books saw the parish paper as a steady source of similar material and wished to have it. Those on the New York staff always made it easy for people to receive sample copies if a full year's subscription was not asked for. Other readers got the magazine at meetings at which Shoemaker spoke. And soon the trifling subscription list—sixty-three at one time, then a few hundred—passed the thousand mark. Perhaps to conserve expense, the rector also slightly changed the format of the magazine, dropped photographs from the covers, and began to use a uniform green cover on each issue, which carried an attractive line drawing of the main entrance of Calvary Church. During the first part of his rectorship, he consistently had one of his younger ordained assistants as the magazine's editor, with the result that, despite the universal appeal of its contents, the magazine remained officially Episcopalian.

But time was moving on. One of his assistants, a Princeton graduate, John P. Cuyler, and a professional journalist, Mrs. James (Peg) Williams, both made creative suggestions as well as valuable contributions to *The Evangel* and the page size was again altered, this time to conform to the dimensions of *Reader's Digest*. For a short time the journal included so much Moral Re-Armament material that it became very much like an American house organ for the Oxford Group, or M.R.A., as this work began to be called. However, the magazine never lost its concern for personal religion and the miracles which the Holy Spirit was ever producing in the lives of individuals.

My own involvement with *The Evangel* came about in a rather roundabout way. The year during which a talented Episcopal priest, Paul Musselman, came on the staff and was asked to assume the editorship of the magazine, saw such a growth of interest in the work of the Oxford Group in America that a team of secretaries was formed to cope with the mass of inquiries being received at "61." I was asked to coordinate this work and take general charge of the small team dealing with this phase of public relations. Sam Shoemaker explained, with no apology, that nothing in the Calvary Church budget could cover my expenses, but that he would like to have me, would make a room available for me at "61" and also have my meals provided for, if I would come and tackle the job. Such a step meant leaving a fairly well-paid post on the staff of a Presbyterian church. This caused me little hesitation, although it seemed a rather unfair deal to my staunchly Christian father whose ire arose, temporarily, at what seemed to him the doubtful prospect of Episcopalians getting the services of a well-trained Presbyterian for free! In due time this question took care of itself, and meanwhile, though still difficult for the head of the Harris household, a most rewarding benefit came my way through the very need of having to live to a large extent on what some call the basis of "faith and prayer." Such a status turned out to be an unusual and extremely valuable adventure.

From the start, while I concentrated on the Oxford Group's inquiry letters, I also made frequent contributions to *The Evangel*. Paul Musselman and I got along well, and his conception of *Evangel* readers as a special "family" of Christians genuinely thrilled me. Paul's own correspondence revealed how much true fellowship could be created between those who had never met face to face, and under his editorship the whole magazine became permeated to a remarkable degree with a genuine family spirit. It also stimulated my imagination to see that, through a new section of excerpts from our incoming letters and by introducing readers' forums and the exchange of news and opinion in the printed word, the equivalent of personal counseling and group meetings could often be reproduced via the printed word. Paul wrote in a lively, humorous fashion and his "Padre's Column," another new magazine feature, became for many the most popular part of the whole journal. He also ferreted out and used the special gifts of those around him. For instance, when he discovered that I had acquired a wealth of pertinent Old Testament material during a year at New College, Edinburgh, he soon had me writing a series of living articles on the lives of Old Testament leaders as they related to our own current times and problems. Thus it came about that the teaching of a dear old Scotsman, Professor Adam Welch, who knew that those "out in front" for Christ had shown forth the faith and courage, the love and justice which our world so sorely lacked, this all came alive through my pen and added still another dimension to the magazine's contents.

Both Paul and I began to correspond with countless overseas subscribers—in England, South Africa, Japan—wherever we found kindred spirits who seemed to have personal spiritual news of their own, asking them to write out their experiences and submit these for possible publication. We explained that we could pay absolutely nothing for such contributions, but we also underlined that a large part of our readership knew that, as with the Bible, the printed page was one of the great agents which God continually used to reach men and to extend His Kingdom. Manuscripts poured in, including innumerable poems, most of which we immediately rejected. But in reality *The Evangel,* as we now called it, was becoming our readers' own magazine.

In 1941, against our vigorous protest, Paul decided to leave the Calvary staff in order to go to M.R.A. as a full-time journalist. I well remember Sam Shoemaker's reluctance to ask me, "a mere Presbyterian," to step into Musselman's shoes. He wasn't at all sure that he wanted a Presbyterian to take over his Episcopal parish publication. In fact, in the very staff meeting in which he announced my appointment as the new editor, this reluctance showed up all too clearly when he said, with a flavor of considerable skepticism, "Well, we will just have to see if Irv can do it." So, in a sense, while I held the post for a long time, I was definitely on trial at the start.

Soon thereafter, with Sam's keen approval, I arranged for a day-long meeting of some whom I felt were maturer Christians than I, friends who had special experience with or a keenness for Christian literature, in order to map out lines of advance. Leslie Glenn came from Washington, and Fred Lawrence, later a Massachusetts bishop, came from Boston. Horace Lukens, who had spent time on *The Evangel* staff, was also present. We pooled our thoughts and discussed with Shoemaker the various directions the magazine might take. No one wanted it to continue to be in part a house organ for M.R.A. In fact, Frank Buchman himself would never have allowed this. We saw that as one alternative we might try to sharpen our wits and create a scholarly publication of a reasonably high intellectual quality, but there already existed so many well-edited journals on theology, church history, and Christian action in the fields of sociology and psychology. No, that wasn't it, nor did anyone advocate letting the magazine become purely parish-centered, however impressive the new life in the parish was becoming. It was the stories of personal religious experience which won the day. These included not only stories of the primary experience of conversion but the further experiences of spiritual growth, including help with Bible study and prayer; experience of genuine fellowship, of which there seemed all too little in the average church; and especially the experience of passing faith on to others and further applying Christian principles in the daily life of businessmen, workers, homemakers, and those in the professions. We prayed a lot that day, and listened, and we listed on paper basic Christian ingredients like the work of the Holy Spirit, in which we believed and on which we felt we should focus. We were happy in our unanimity and in the knowledge that we were expressing some of the hopes of the early editors as well as setting a high goal for ourselves. We also became aware that we would be meeting a need in the field of Christian journalism by making available a periodical which was avowedly centered on Christian experience. Was not faith simply our belief in action under God? How could man find a more living faith that could at once be put into action? As Sam continued to repeat that we should make clear that "Christianity is a religion that works," we felt we saw our way. And we coined a subtitle for the publication: *The Magazine of Christian Experience.*

The first issues I undertook to bring out filled this then young man's heart with zest and joy. Material of the kind we wanted was ample. At first plenty of mistakes appeared. In one instance a whole page of copy got misplaced. But we soon discovered that such mishaps came chiefly from our failure to arrange with the printer for such essentials as page proofs. Errors were graciously overlooked, and a universal spirit of optimism pervaded the whole work and was reflected in our correspondence. This became so heavy as to present us with our first major problem. We still had neither a regular business manager nor even a secretary. Organizationally, we registered little but weakness; but as a small, devoted team we possessed "what it takes."

Needs were answered in curious ways. A young woman who typed all day in a Wall Street office offered to stop by Calvary House twice a week at 5:15 if I would stay over and give her my most urgent dictation. Stay over! I told Vera Bagley that she could find me in the office at almost any hour, night or day—a slight exaggeration. So the friends who had sent remittances from Kalamazoo or subscription lists from Johannesburg began to get attention. And the experience I had received in editing the *Princeton Alumni Weekly* bore fruit of another kind. My ability to scan manuscripts, my familiarity with various type faces, and my knowledge of how to use the semicolon and the hyphen paid off immediately in conserved time and fairly competent editing. And my days in Scotland had given me a nose for heresy.

One day a horse and wagon carted a perfectly proportioned old table all the way to Gramercy Park from a downtown office to supply the need for an editorial and layout unit. More important, a retired engineer in Summit, New Jersey, Alec Beck, who had a facile pen and a fund of knowledge of church history, offered to commute to the city five days a week and assist with rewrites and other editorial chores. Within a year he persuaded his younger brother, John, to offer to become an assistant editor, volunteering his services without any financial compensation except his out-of-pocket expenses for carfare and luncheons. Not long after this, Helen Shoemaker spotted a wonderfully able young business executive, a member of the parish and already in the publishing field with a firm that was planning to move out of the city. This was Bertha Elliott, who, wishing to remain in New York and believing in what we had undertaken, was persuaded to become the business manager of *The Evangel* at a salary greatly below what she had been receiving. Bertha brought to our office that steady, loving professional contribution we so badly needed. Organizer par excellence, gracious hostess, and expert proofreader, she became the mainstay of so much that lay ahead. Over the years she also found many volunteers to help with our growing clerical work in the business office. At the same time she found an ever-increasing number of Americans to sponsor and underwrite the subscriptions of Christians overseas who wanted *The Evangel* but found it increasingly difficult, especially during war time, to send in their own subscription remittances.

It was not long before I found myself devoting at least one day a week entirely to correspondence. It wasn't so much the business details whose growing demands pressed upon me. Bertha dealt with the preponderance of that work and always personalized it with special little messages from one who obviously cared about those to whom she was writing. No, my concern focused in two other facts: the steadily growing number of correspondents whose faith made it possible to include them as teammates at the center of the *Evangel* family and, secondly, the obvious loneliness and need which showed between the lines of many incoming letters. I began to see that, as my friend and classmate Ray Purdy had already told me, the most important aspect of our correspondence lay in the fact that many letters represented a God-given touch with people whom we might well be able to help spiritually."Don't try to answer all their questions. Understand and meet their personal needs." Then, too, in the New York office we had the names and addresses of people in every section of the country, many of whom were already participating in family and home groups in which new friends could be included. Other out-of-town friends could be looked to for spiritual counseling; and often all it took on our part to furnish help was to give a new subscriber an introduction to such a person. After a year or two we developed a kind of network across the United States and Canada and had cards conveniently at hand which listed a couple of hundred individuals we knew well enough to use as contact people for those looking for fellowship and counseling. It proved great fun to hear that: "Yes, Leo Hall, in Michigan, was now linked up with a men's weekly meeting in a church in his area"; or that John Karefa-Smart of Sierra Leone, soon after entering McGill Medical School, had become active with older business men like Will Goodwin and Arthur Paterson at St. Edward's Church, Montreal. And so on and so on.

In one special instance, we promptly referred to an English physician, Dr. Jim Bell Nicholl (who had himself found faith at Lee Abbey, an Anglican conference center in North Devon), a woman who wrote to us from the British Midlands. She wrote that an *Evangel* article had been the instrument of keeping her from an intended suicide. She had been tearing up a copy of the magazine to stuff paper into the chinks of her kitchen window before turning on the gas, when the title of an article struck her eye. It read "It May Be Your Stomach!" She sat down, read the article, decided to postpone her destructive plan and see if she could contact the British medical man referred to in the story. They met, she became his patient and then a twice-born child of God. At Harvest Festival she gratefully drove to his home to provide him and his family with a turkey dinner.

Various New Yorkers saw the possibilities and worked with us. For instance, two friends, Tom and Blanche Page, sent an extra copy of *The Evangel* to Gert Behanna in Chicago as a follow-up of the dinner-table conversation described elsewhere. This issue printed a Shoemaker article entitled "It's Never Too Late" which, as a follow-up of Tom's witness, carried Gert to her knees where she received the power to live a new life that afterwards affected thousands of others through her autobiography, *The Late Liz*, her countless speaking engagements, and a famous recording, "God Is Not Dead."

In *The Evangel* office we also learned to carry on locally whatever activities we recommended to our readers. Since we believed in and wrote about group meetings, we all became actively involved in such groups ourselves. And the same with larger, "witness" meetings and week-end conferences; we initiated and conducted these as a staff before we wrote about them in the magazine. One of our most fruitful experiments became a Thursday afternoon tea when, at 4:30, work was cleared away and visitors of many sorts were welcomed in the editors' office. Bertha carried this plan through to perfection. There was always time to talk as well as eat, and it was at these teas that we came to meet and to know such great souls as Norman and Pauline Grubb, as well as those from farther afield like Dr. and Mrs. D. T. Niles of Ceylon and Chaplain Peter Takeda from Tokyo, Japan.

As the magazine grew, we discovered a wealth of specially talented people among our own readership—artists, photographers, and feature writers. Notable among these was Jim Ashbrook of Philadelphia whose Christmas and Easter covers, so beautifully designed and lettered, created a special market for these issues that ran into the thousands. John Beck provided us with striking action shots which formed the basis of three specially illustrated, yearly supplements that added greatly to the interest in the magazine. And Ted Robinson in Binghamton, New York, whom we came to know through Bruce Larson, contributed black-and-white drawings of *Evangel* writers so accurate, beautiful, and lifelike that we used his pictures of well-known authors like Ralston Young and Sam Shoemaker over and over again, both to identify articles and also to enliven the magazine pages.

Jackson Abbott, official illustrator of the Pennsylvania Fish and Game Commission, also served us freely and in a uniquely important way with his charming pictures of the animals featured in a series of *Evangel* children's stories by Dorothy Bennett. Such keen interest arose in "Flora Fox and Her Friends," partly because of Jack's drawings, that our only fully illustrated paperback came out one Christmas and by the following December had been reproduced, colors and all, in pre-Communist China.

The demand for extra copies of some of our articles became so insistent that we developed a plan to make many of these available in reprint form. Furthermore, nothing was copyrighted, so articles were often reprinted in sister magazines. Others were unexpectedly translated into foreign languages, and for several years a quarterly known as *The Tokyo Evangel* appeared in Japan and secured a very large subscription list there, one which far surpassed the number of copies we were printing in the United States.

Chapter 8 tells the story of Bernie Gair, a deeply converted teacher with a Hebraic background, vice principal of the Alexander Hamilton High School in Brooklyn. It's amusing to add here that his original story, a 1600-word article called "Discovery," was translated within a couple of years into French, German, Spanish, and modern Greek, while a neat folder presenting it in Yiddish rolled off a press in New York City to the tune of 20,000 copies.

"An Outline of the Life of Christ," authored by Helen Shoemaker and Irving Harris, had appeared in pamphlet form during Calvary's Oxford Group days, and this, plus the demand for other magazine articles, gave us the idea of arranging with our printer for the publication of a series of paperbacks, or what used to be called pocket books. John Beck found the time to start the ball rolling with a 96-page illustrated booklet in a bright red cover which we called *God Has the Answer*, and the availability of some of our "cream of the crop" material in fresh, inexpensive form proved popular. (For many years these books cost only 25¢ each.) The most ambitious of these paperbacks, *What it Takes!*, appeared during World War II and was edited expressly for young men and women in the armed forces. Our several American printings were supplemented by Canadian and Australian editions, and both here and abroad copies circulated in defense plants as well as among the forces. The chief of chaplains of the United States Army ordered sample copies to be sent to all the chaplains under his command, while the manager of a war defense plant in Long Island City had thousands of free copies distributed to the employees in his huge factory. At Gramercy Park we soon began to receive visits as well as letters from a whole new crowd of younger people in uniform and from blue-collar workers in the metropolitan area. One of the latter, by the way, was Ellis Van Riper, now known in labor circles as a top official of the AFL-CIO Transport Workers Union, who in the days of our first contacts was shoveling coal in a power plant in Manhattan. His fellowship in Calvary House meetings with men like Edward M. Cabaniss and J. C. Penney illustrated the profitable way *Evangel* literature and groups were furnishing a common Christian meeting ground for Americans of varying backgrounds.

Then there were the "pen friends," starting with an isolated Alaskan Eskimo who found the names and addresses in the magazine itself, and other Christians with whom correspondence proved an enriching experience. Thus, without consciously planning it that way, the magazine became really more of a fellowship than a publication, and most of those responsible in any way for its production felt its family spirit was truly accomplishing the extension of God's Kingdom here on earth.

As inflation pushed us, especially through the typographers union's demands on the Sowers Printing Company, we had to reduce the number of yearly issues from twelve to ten and then from ten to eight; but the number of pages and subscribers, and the quality of the publication itself, we believe, continued to increase and increase. We resisted making the magazine appear too slick and too commercial, although we did start looking for and finding a few advertisements, chiefly those of book publishers. And we began using photographs of people on our covers.

As far as I know everyone who participated in these publishing ventures, including the printer, sooner or later found the experience an exhilarating adventure. Personally, I came to hate deadlines and, becoming physically exhausted, sometimes wanted an out. Occasionally I wondered whether periodicals with their inevitable pressures represented work fully pleasing to God. But on the other hand, even some Calvary vestrymen who had been unsympathetic to Sam Shoemaker's ecumenical work in general, and *The Evangel* in particular, came eventually—with but one exception—to cheer loudly for our magazine and offer suggestions. In this era many businessmen and bankers expected to work on Saturday mornings. William H. Deatly, president of the Title Guarantee Company of lower Broadway, volunteered such time for free, first to tackle the parish accounts and then, since we couldn't afford an accountant, to work on the ledgers of *The Evangel*, submitting monthly reports to help out the cause. His sparkling financial genius was ours for the taking. Later, when at long last we were forced to leave Gramercy Park, it was another vestryman, J. Daire van Cott who, with a fellow lawyer, Ludlow Fowler of St. James Church, got us incorporated as a nonprofit organization, all without charging us a nickel. Bill and Daire became founding members of Faith at Work, Inc., the magazine's new owner.

11/
Red Cap 42—
Bishop of Grand Central

In the murky atmosphere of a September evening a chill was
settling over the approaches to New York's Grand Central Station.
Ralston Young had about decided to hop the subway for Harlem
and home when he heard one of the head porters shout, "'Doc'
you better take a look out there." Reluctantly he stepped through a
door onto the taxi ramp for incoming baggage and at once saw a tall
woman standing alone on the sidewalk with a pile of heavy luggage around her. Two other porters stood motionless in the
shadows, obviously not intending to lend a hand. The woman's
taxi had disappeared.

Red Cap 42 reached for a hand-truck and, walking toward the
stranded traveler, said, "Lady, can I help you?"

Turning, the woman uttered a sigh of relief and said in an English accent, "Oh, thank you very much. There's been some
mistake. I'm trying to reach the Baltimore and Ohio Railroad
Station somewhere on 42nd Street but my time is running out and
I'm not at all sure where I am."

"Don't worry, Ma'am." Ralston swung the canvas-covered bags
onto his truck and pointed toward Vanderbilt Avenue. Then he
smiled. "I'll get you there in plenty of time. The B. & O. terminal
is just around the corner."

As the redcap pushed the luggage out under the street lights, the
slender woman followed along. At the corner of 42nd Street she

said nervously, "It's so very important for me to reach the other station on time."

"Yes 'um." Ralston nodded but kept the truck moving.

"You see I'm a new secretary on the British delegation to the UN," the woman continued. "It would be unthinkable to arrive late on my first assignment in the States."

"Yeah, that sounds mighty important," answered the redcap. "But you know, when I feel upset the way you do now, I take a deep breath and remember what Jesus Christ once said, 'Come unto me all ye that labor and are heavy laden and I will give you rest.'"

At this the woman stopped short. "What was that you said?"

Ralston stopped too. "I just mean that when I get excited on the job," he explained, "I try to remember Jesus Christ and put my faith to work."

Above the noise of the traffic he could hear the woman gasp. Then they proceeded. At a spot by the Commodore Hotel the redcap stopped again, unloaded the truck, and pointed across the street at the brightly lighted entrance to the B. & O. station. When a gap appeared between the stream of cars, he motioned to his customer and they crossed over, the English woman walking briskly at his side.

Inside the B. & O. waiting room a crowd was bustling about. Once the woman was seated, the redcap and the bags disappeared through a door. When he emerged he had baggage checks and a ticket in his hand.

"There you are," he said laughing. "Now you really should hop on the bus there. It connects with your train in Jersey City. You've got a nice ride through the Holland Tunnel. And don't worry about the bags. They'll be returned to you in Washington."

By this time the woman was also smiling. To Ralston she looked like a different person. "Thank you so very much, porter. But what should I give you?"

"Nothing," Young replied emphatically. "Just the railroad's charges, 25¢ a bag."

"Nothing! But there must be a tip." Somewhat confused, the woman fumbled in her bag and came up with a $1 bill. As she handed him the dollar she grasped his hand. "Porter, you'll never know how much I owe you. You're the first, the very first person I've talked to in America, and you've not only helped me catch my train, you've said things that make me feel ashamed of myself. I *call* myself a Christian but what you've said has shown me I'm way off my course. Thank you. . . . Thank you so very much."

And with that she was gone.

As the redcap retrieved his truck, he slowly put the dollar into his pocket. At 25¢ a bag, the dollar—a "lamb's tongue" in redcap parlance—would all go to the New York Central. "So what!" Ralston said to himself. "This is just a great way to end the day. What that lady said to me was surely the best tip I've had in a long while."

*   *   *

Ralston Crosbie Young was born in Panama on November 22, 1896, and came to the States about twenty years later to work in the nation's shipyards. World War I was reaching a climax, with the allies unrelentingly pursuing their hideous slugfest in the trenches in France. The dearth of American transports needed to supplement great British troopships like the ill fated *Majestic* was putting the heat on every ship builder on the East Coast. Wages had soared and muscular young men had little difficulty in landing jobs in one of the several shipyards around Newark Bay or in some other spot near the Metropolitan area of New York.

With some friends Ralston located work in a yard on Staten Island and at the same time took a room in a boardinghouse in Harlem. It was a strenuous life but he sweated away happily for many months with the satisfying sense that he was serving his country and also securing a future for his family, still in Panama. While a very young boy, he had lost his father. That was about the time that General Goethals was dynamiting the Culebra Mountains. Ralston was the oldest child, so from then on he had felt a special responsibility for his mother and the others at home.

In 1918, when everything was working out happily, *wham*!—the war was suddenly over and his particular shipyard all but shut down overnight.

With his meager education Ralston realized that he was no match for the thousands of returning soldiers when it came to locating a new job. Large numbers of our troops had high-school or college diplomas, and whole battalions of these men were equipped to fit immediately into the commercial life of our cities.

With his last pay check in his pocket, the future redcap set out and searched frantically for work, but well-paid jobs were nonexistent. In order to survive, he and his friends washed dishes in Times Square restaurants and got employment cleaning floors and loading trucks. Absolutely nothing better came their way, nothing that paid wages even approaching what they had made in the shipyards.

At first Ralston was irritated, then anxious and humiliated. However, despite the utter confusion of the winter which followed the Armistice, he kept going, staying on in the rooming house in Harlem and setting his face against the easier option of leaving New York. An unusually optimistic disposition kept him thinking positively. Other inherited gifts, plus his family upbringing and church training, had endowed him with an almost unconscious faith in God's providence. If he could have put his philosophy into words, it might have been summed up in a sentence or two he used later with unbelieving individuals in Grand Central, "Man, listen! God has a plan for your life."

One wintry afternoon, business in the Station Master's office at Grand Central Station was humming. As a batch of applications from men seeking employment as redcaps was being processed, an alert New York Central clerk came upon two men, either of whom might well fill a vacancy among the station's large number of black porters. The force in those days numbered several hundred. Strangely enough, both applications had been endorsed by a New York Central vice president, and both applicants, as far as the clerk could tell, met the necessary qualifications as to age, residence, and general fitness. For some obscure reason that Ralston never understood he and not the other man was chosen, although the latter had once worked for the railroad official who had okayed both applications. A slip of paper arrived shortly by mail notifying him that he had been accepted as a station porter and assigned a relatively low number. From then on, for better or for worse, he became "Red Cap 42."

The news came as a relief but caused him little elation. To don a uniform and serve people "in work clothes like—well, like a servant" was hardly his idea of a good reason for having left Panama, and he realized that his new job would lack the zest of the strenuous work in a shipyard. Besides, working as a redcap in 1919 (and straight through the twenties) meant being on duty in the station

ten hours a day with only one day off every two weeks. Furthermore, believe it or not, there was no salary. Those who made up
this huge force of mainly high-quality public servants depended
for their living entirely on tips.

Ralston poignantly remembers the morning when he found
himself pushing an elderly woman in a wheelchair across the main
concourse. The menial nature of this new work suddenly filled
him with disgust. That noon he told his friends that he was going
to quit. But somehow he never did. Instead, as the days went by,
he developed a grim determination to keep the unpleasant job
indefinitely. He shopped around the clothes emporiums of Harlem, took in the sights when off duty, and soon began to enjoy the
fellowship of the redcaps' locker room. After the inner refusal to
sail for home, the tenor of life improved, but he still remained
deeply dissatisfied.

A few months passed. With increasing savvy about Harlem's
rooming facilities, he located the kind of a building in which he
could rent an apartment suitable as a permanent home—suitable
for his mother, too, if she decided to come North. He was "an edgy
buck" with a chip on his shoulder and a blurred sense of unde-
served injustice. These characteristics marked what he calls his
"B.C." days, and he will tell you that he has never been very
proud of them. But at the same time he possessed a strong, built-in
conscience which the bright lights of the city never seriously
dulled. In fact he soon became fed up with merely putting on new
clothes and "playing around."

An elderly woman of his own race finally proved to be an "open
sesame" into an entirely different life. My, how she annoyed him
at first, coming every Sunday morning into the building where he
lived in order to pick up a couple of youngsters and cart them off to
Sunday School. It mystified Ralston that she seemed to like to do
this—seemed to love children. After a while, he became uncon-
trollably curious and stopped her one Sunday to ask her to explain.
Yes, he said as they talked, he knew St. Philip's Church and how
close it was to his apartment. The woman spoke most warmly of
Shelton Hale Bishop, the rector, and said that besides having one
of the best Sunday Schools in New York City, he also ran a day-
school during the week, with a playgound for younger children to
keep them off the crowded streets.

There came a Sunday morning soon afterwards when Ralston

Young put his newspaper aside and dressed up in his very best. Sharp at eleven he was at St. Philip's and soon happily worshipping in the very way he was accustomed to in Panama. He fumbled a little with his Prayer Book—the liturgy seemed slightly altered—but he felt a glow in participating in the service as if somehow he had come home. But it was the sermon that got him. The man in the pulpit seemed to be talking to no one in the vast congregation but himself. On the porch going out he shook hands and asked the preacher if he could come to see him.

Priest and porter met two or three days later, and in their unhurried hour together it was as if a window to heaven opened to Ralston. He considered it a turning point in his life. The older man, though ordained, completely disarmed him at the very start of their conversation by leveling with him and explaining that, almost daily, he was still conscious of a need of God's forgiveness. He became very specific as they talked on, and very encouraging, too, especially about the release and forgiveness which he claimed God was offering every man. Ralston walked home on air, humbled as rarely before but as joyful as a songbird.

Then at Shelton Bishop's suggestion, Ralston saw Sam Shoemaker. Once again he felt the truth of the liberating secret of simple openness. As in Harlem, so in Gramercy Park. He met someone who was quite honest with him, and it was natural to be honest in return—honest about his own ill will and resentment, his pride, and the impurity which had marked his New York life prior to the preceding Sunday. Sam and he saw each other as kindred spirits, and as they talked, the breeze of the Spirit touched them and the Lordship of Jesus Christ was reaffirmed in Ralston's heart as never before. When asked later about these two redemptive interviews, he would explain with a chuckle, "I just opened up the carpet sweeper—and we had prayer."

As was his way with any New Yorker, the rector of Calvary Church urged Red Cap 42 to look in on our Monday afternoon men's meeting. "If you come off your job by three or four, you'll be just in time. Walk through the church, if you wish, and when it's five-thirty you'll find other fellows like yourself right here on the second floor of Calvary House."

So there Ralston stood one Monday, the upper portion of his red cap covered by a neat, black cloth, and in a rather relaxed way ready for anything. Actually few men ever fitted into this Monday group more easily, and those of us who formed the core of the weekly meetings will ever remember the first few times he participated with us.

Ralston had his own way of characterizing such fellowship. To other redcaps he simply said that the meeting on Gramercy Park was the place where he went to keep his feet to the fire. And as Bruce Larson was to put it later on, it was at Calvary House that he saw what it meant, as a Christian, to have "a growing edge."

A year passed during which Ralston found a place in our smaller planning group in an upstairs room where two or three of us regularly welcomed seasoned early-comers in order to consider the basic and relevant New Testament principles which would give the "open" meetings progressive, Bible-centered direction. Here we heard progress reports from various people, and we realized what a variety of activities Ralston was engaging in at the station. One day, for example, he laughingly told how he had steered an alcoholic customer away from a bar to nearby toy and candy counters. "You don't need another drink," he had suggested to one man, "but maybe the children at home would like a present." He explained that he had learned to "carry passengers' burdens as well as their bags."

The following Christmas he found a blackboard in the locker room and chalked up the verse: "Unto Thee a Child Is Given." A little later he began referring to the station as the place where he needed special help. "That's where I'm naughty, where I still get irritated and lose my temper." He would laugh as he said this, but we knew that lack of fellowship on the job troubled him. Someone suggested that he form an off-shoot group up in Harlem, and he was ready to do that. But what he most wanted was a group of friends right where he worked, right where he spent a good part of six days a week. "The station's the place," he quietly maintained, "but I wouldn't know where to meet. The locker room itself is out. No one but redcaps are allowed in there."

They say that God works in mysterious ways His wonders to perform, and what happened next was indeed a wonder. Soon after Easter that year, an author, an architect, an editor, and a redcap were seen sitting huddled close together in a corner of the high-backed, mahogany bench which runs around the walls of Grand Central's vast waiting room. There we were at half-past ten to the minute: Harvard's "poet laureate," Hermann Hagedorn; and next to him a top architect of the old Ritz-Carlton Hotel, Desmond Upton; the third was the editor of *The Calvary Evangel;* and finally there was Ralston Young. The latter had come straight from his early luncheon and he offered to moderate the informal meeting. We were slightly self-conscious, aware of passersby, loungers, and the murmuring noise of the traveling public. Ralston suggested that we sit a moment in silence and wait. Somewhere a train announcer was rattling off his resonant patter. But we were not waiting for this. At last one man spoke briefly, then another. The architect, an alcoholic, told of his efforts to channel caring into his home life. Ralston described the difficulties of being at everybody's beck and call. Finally at his suggestion we bowed our heads and quietly repeated the Lord's Prayer. All told, we had spent only half an hour.

This group became another weekly New York fixture, and as the meetings continued they acted as a purifying gateway for visitors headed for our pleasure-centered city. As time passed, a school teacher, a businessman from across Forty-second Street, and several subscribers to *The Calvary Evangel* all learned in that waiting room to slough off their self-consciousness and take new steps for God. "Tuesdays at 10:30" merrily continued for over a year until, through a further minor miracle—and at the suggestion of an elevator operator from the adjacent Graybar Building—Track 13 opened its welcoming, more adequate arms and gave the meetings the privacy which a waiting room could never offer. Here the unlighted section of an early morning passenger train idled away several hours daily, close to the entrance gate.

With the hearty approval of the station master, Ralston decided to convene his meetings on Track 13, changing the hour to noon for the convenience of those who wished to come. Children might have called the place spooky, for only a greenish glimmer of light from the few fixtures high above the platform penetrated the coaches. But once inside the car—always the second from the rear end of the train—the moderator's hearty greetings and contagious laughter drew visitors up the aisle to a location where Ralston had turned over the backs of two double seats to provide comfortable space for those who arrived early. And as at Gramercy Park, most of those who attended quickly sensed that here they were privileged to experience the personal Presence of Almighty God—something more than a chance merely to talk about Him.

Under these circumstances, it was not surprising that, after a month or two, the group multiplied threefold, resulting in meetings every Monday, Wednesday, and Friday.

* * *

Since *The Evangel* was now printing stories about, or by, Red Cap 42 two or three times a year, a good many readers started asking questions about the Grand Central meetings. "How does one find Ralston Young in the station?" was asked by commuters and casual travelers alike. "On what days does he hold his groups?" Suddenly such interest intensified, for news of Track 13 broke in a big way through the February 1946 *Reader's Digest* in an article by Sam Shoemaker. The first version of this gem of a story was drafted for the *Digest's* "Most Unforgettable Character" series by Fulton Oursler, their senior editor on matters religious. Mr. Oursler, a friend and admirer of Calvary's rector, had planned to write a longer story describing features of Shoemaker's many-sided ministry in Gramercy Park, but prior to the composition of this he was persuaded by a young resident at Calvary House, who was a member of the new Clergy School there, to investigate the outreach of the Gramercy Park work by viewing "the latest, most novel example of creating Christian cells."

The day the eminent editor came to the station a divine stage manager must have set the scene, for in a dark corner at the rear of the coach Ralston was using, an individual in grimy overalls was fast asleep, quite oblivious to what was happening and unnoticed by those attending the Track 13 meeting. At the very moment when Mr. Oursler was marveling at the quietness of a spot so close to moving trains and the surface roar of Park Avenue traffic, the proceedings were suddenly punctuated by a loud and wonderfully uninhibited snore. The author, highly amused, quietly decided then and there that instead of a report on Gramercy Park he would make Red Cap 42 the substance of his story. Sam was delighted to edit and sign the article.

As early copies of the magazine hit the newsstands of the city they caused an immediate stir. Coming as the article did on the heels of the twentieth century's second worldwide war, the picture it gave seemed to many readers a vivid, joyful contrast to recent headlines. To more than a few New Yorkers the story sounded like the all-clear signal of the old air-raid siren. It caught the attention of people of all ages and was soon noticed 'round the world. Fan mail began arriving at the *Digest's* Pleasantville, New York, office; at Calvary House; and even at Grand Central Station itself. The first letters Sam brought into The *Evangel* office at "61" were written by New York residents and commuters; some had Long Island and Westchester postmarks. But the most significant correspondence only reached us after a month or so, for such letters came from men and women who had been fighting with the allied forces overseas.

All in all, this correspondence spoke volumes about the effectiveness of a faith that works and the mysterious way the Almighty was using an obscure person in New York, plus the black type of the printed word.

A significant step in Ralston Young's life and in his career as a religious speaker and Christian leader was his marriage to Sadie Morgan of Greenville, North Carolina, in 1941. When he accepted an invitation to spend a short holiday in the South at the home of another redcap's parents, matrimony was still a side issue, although no one could have called him indifferent to the other sex. Meeting Sadie was like the happy surprises which mark the progress of many men of goodwill. Their chance acquaintance quickly became a warm, intimate relationship and, since both were in their thirties, a long engagement would have been silly.

Sadie knew the North and had already enjoyed the hospitality of friends in Princeton, New Jersey. When she came North again and made her appearance at St. Philip's Church and Calvary as Ralston's wife, she was given a gay and hearty reception. At first the couple lived in Harlem and Sadie made her secretarial skills and experiences useful in an office at Seabury House, headquarters of the Episcopal Church, at that time only a block from Gramercy Park. Without the slightest reservation she participated with Ralston in all of his church activities except those specifically pertaining to men's work, and was sometimes introduced as "Mrs. Red Cap 42"—an extremely appropriate and well meant compliment.

In the second or third year of their marriage, they crossed the Hudson and moved into a charming little house in the village of Vauxhall near Milburn and Short Hills, New Jersey, and this home, like several belonging to suburbanites who were active in the outreach work of Calvary House, became a beehive of spiritual activity. Following the usual pattern of those in *The Calvary Evangel* fellowship, as well as their own inclinations, the Youngs made their local church a priority, serving on committees—though at the time they were the only Negroes in the congregation—and entertaining fellow parishioners in their new home.

*   *   *

For several years a team of fifteen or twenty of us had been setting aside one Saturday a month for the kind of creative fellowship which insured personal, spiritual growth and gave direction to current evangelistic programs. We met in one another's homes and Ralston and Sadie began to share their house. The ample time before and after lunch provided a chance for us to speak frankly about our personal and family needs, to engage in prayer—much spoken, some silent—and to seek, through hard thinking and meditation, direction for our daily lives, both as individuals and as a team. Before dispersing, we would often pair off, two by two, to clear relationships and, if necessary, to seek help with personal problems—those knotty, stubborn "Achilles heel" kind of weaknesses which cause spiritual dryness and division if repressed.

At these Saturday "picnics" we also wrestled with serious social issues. When school desegregation became the order of the day, we spent more than one Saturday afternoon considering racial conditions as we knew them and studying references in the New Testament which pinpointed America's sins, including complacency, as well as policies of which we could be proud. Since our team was interracial we had at least a few solutions operating in our own homes and in the churches we represented.

Speaking from his own experiences in the alternating quiet and turmoil of the station, Ralston more than once described improvements already discernible in his daily occupation. "Of course," he admitted ruefully, "a few folks always try to upset the apple cart, but I see so much that's different in America from what we took for granted just a few years ago. Why just yesterday in the station . . ." and he was off, giving us chapter and verse about some change in a racially difficult social situation which had resulted from the change in one person's heart. "People say that human nature can't be changed, but I see the change happening almost every day. God will have His way. He will have the last word if we let Him."

That was a basic part of Ralston's creed and when he expressed it he spoke for the whole team.

*　　*　　*

After Sam Shoemaker left New York and, as Faith at Work, Inc., we had opened an office at 8 West 40th Street, near the Public Library, Ralston would frequently send people over to either our Tuesday men's meeting or one of Bertha Elliott's office teas. As a staff, we thus made new friends among the traveling public, many of whom wanted to know more about cell groups and how faith could answer their personal problems. We, in turn, would suggest to out-of-town and overseas subscribers who visited the office that their stay in New York would not be complete unless they spent an hour on Track 13. We were entertaining magazine readers from places as distant as Taiwan and Japan and as crucial to America's foreign policy as Western Germany, and the exchange between office and station proved happy and profitable. A committee of leading industrialists from the Orient told us that Red Cap 42 was the one American they most desired to meet, and a like statement was made by a learned Scottish professor from Edinburgh.

Not too much later, news that sounded incredible except to his fellow porters and a few close friends spread through the grapevine: "Ralston Young is retiring." Why should there have been advance notice? It was a mandatory matter based on age, bringing to an end Ralston's more than forty years with the New York Central Railroad. The Track 13 meetings would naturally end too, and a host of friends shook their heads and wondered if anything but a quiet, conventional retirement could follow for Ralston and Sadie Young.*

But far from it! Before his famous red cap could be put on the

---

* In the winter of 1977, the Youngs took one of their periodic trips to Canada. Sadie Young returned with a miserable cold and on January 4, 1978, "Mrs. Red Cap 42" passed on. Ralston's sense of loneliness was intense but the fellowship he had always given others returned to him twice-fold. A Philadelphia friend invited him to visit Jamaica, B.W.I. On his return he 'phoned me: "I've never felt so bereft, but Sadie is closer to me now than ever. I'll not be weeping for her again. She is in that better land where she wants to be and we'll be together soon."

shelf, an invitation reached him from his old church in Harlem. Would he go on St. Philip's staff as a minister of visitation to call on members in their homes and extend the church's services to the sick? It was an important task and Ralston greatly admired the younger rector now in charge there. But he hesitated. He loved the immense, needy Harlem parish, but another parish lay even closer to his heart, one without specified boundaries but whose every building and landmark he knew almost as well as he knew his own name. It was the bustling business district of East Forty-second Street, that part of Manhattan of which the great station where he had spent his working life formed the hub, what most New Yorkers referred to as "the Grand Central area." Here were streets and offices teeming with people with whom he felt a strange, strong, personal bond. Several members of the Faith at Work staff were among the numerous New Yorkers who understood. A few of these speculated on the feasibility of forming a local, retail outlet for the larger work of Faith at Work, which had become national in scope, and someone suggested the rather startling name of "The Manhattan Project." The thinking here was simply that if America's wartime leadership had created the terrible atom bomb through a research project known as "The Manhattan Project," would it not be possible for other Americans to redeem the name and set up a framework within which the *spiritual* bombs which had marked Ralston's ministry might, under God, continue in production? Ralston Crosbie Young, now ex-Red Cap 42, waxed enthusiastic, and when an enterprising member of the Faith at Work board of directors secured the permission of the city fathers of New York to use the appellation for a nonprofit organization to carry on activities "to teach and advance the Christian faith," a lively weekly group at once began, the visible heir of the responsibilities and operations of the gatherings on Track 13.

We first used a small office at 295 Madison Avenue in a towering building, only a stone's throw from Grand Central, into which Faith at Work, Inc. itself had recently moved, and we had the copyright of the name registered in Albany. Someone donated a secondhand desk. A complete stranger, a man in the furniture business, hearing of the new Manhattan Project and liking the idea, sent in twelve folding chairs. A coat locker and a kitchen table appeared from a more mysterious source. A week later, surrounded by a stack of blue earthenware cups and saucers, a sugar bowl and a can of powdered milk, an ex-redcap was brewing coffee in his new office.

Visitors soon deluged the tiny quarters. A men's group was set for Tuesdays at noon and a Bible class slated for Thursdays at 4:30 P.M. Thus the elevators at 295 brought strangers up from the ground floor and Faith at Work staff personnel and friends down from the tower offices above. Sandwiches in paper bags became familiar at the noon meetings, and but for the hardness of the wooden chairs it was Track 13 all over again, with Ralston's familiar chuckle constantly punctuating the proceedings.

When pressed for an explanation, the one-time redcap with mock seriousness would simply say that when his days had run out at the station, Someone of great influence had provided him with a Madison Avenue office!

Since then, as moderator, coordinator, secretary in various, changing locations, including the Williams Club and the office of a Madison Avenue advertising company, Ralston Young has joyfully carried on. As he goes and comes on trains and buses, or attends a weekend conference at a church, the quiet, loving power of the redcap-that-was continues to catch on. A "new man" ever and again makes another new man, to make still another new man in what scientists call a chain reaction. Ralston's quality of life is truly "the salt of the earth" and the yeast of the bread called fellowship.

And the end? I would say that such a ministry has no end. It is too full of the eternal verities. It creates too much fun. Ralston as we see him in the flesh will fade away. But this he has been doing for years, letting self fade so that other people may come into the light. He has already lost part of the life with which he started, but day by day he is clearly finding a brand new one.

12 /

Alone in the Dark—
Communist Turns Christian*

*T*he stark realities of New York City's Third Avenue in the old days of the streetcar and the whirring, overhead elevated trains depressed many who encountered them. Life rushed along, nearly always noisy and, in its personal aspects, often grim, if not sordid.

Picture a small, grubby house with a Communist couple living and joking—and before long fighting—with each other on the top floor. Grace Lumpkin had come to New York from the South where she had seen enough racial conflict and individual brutality to sow within her the seeds of radicalism. When she joined a group of other young girls in eking out a meager living by a variety of operations connected with a Quaker-controlled magazine, she acquired more than a job. Linked as the Quakers were with pacificism, and "violently" promoting social justice, equable race relations, and fair wages, the journal had already acquired a decided left-wing slant. As the pendulum swung ever farther in the socialist direction, Miss Lumpkin and her clique gladly swung with it, sometimes unwittingly, often enthusiastically.

Grace's first assignment placed her in the subscription department. Surely no lack of need in this area! The girls she worked

---

*The final part of this chapter is a rewritten version of an *Evangel* story, reprinted with permission from *Guideposts*, Pawling, New York.

with were different from any she had ever known. There was Rose, "a regular whirlwind," who solicited advertisements and helped with the make-up. Marsha was a Russian anarchist married to a fellow revolutionary. Julita, a Spanish anarchist living with but not married to (for such cults did not necessarily approve of marriage) another left-winger. Felicia, a Negro girl, had a quiet voice, a beautifully shaped head, and an extremely dark skin. Sophy was an out-and-out Communist, and Jane, another Negro, light of skin, very pretty, always pert, and laughing most of the time, was some kind of a socialist.

Rose set the pace for the whole outer office, but each of the girls who had political beliefs tried to convert her, not to Quakerism but to the various brands of political convictions they respectively believed in. And for a time Grace Lumpkin enjoyed the scene, looked upon the group as curious, interesting, and likable, and exposed herself to a stiff if liberal education.

Having never worked in an office before, Grace found she was slow in mastering details and conscientiously stayed long after five o'clock to complete her stint for the day. For this she received little notice from the editors but much abuse from her new friends who objected to her kow-towing to "the bosses." Here existed the basis for her first solid conflict; she liked the girls and respected their opinions, but she also felt "the bosses" had been more than good in providing adequate pay and at the same time great freedom. The conflict led to hours of discussion and also to a certain amount of research. Grace went to the sources and read Marx and Lenin. She enjoyed her life and abandoned her strict discipline, but underneath she always had a gnawing, uneasy feeling that she was going back on the best she knew.

It became easy to neglect any expression of faith and worship, and for a time she fell into the general ridicule and criticism of religion among the group. However, in reading Lenin, she found two areas she had to dub blind spots in what he wrote: (1) he avowedly set out to prove that everything connected with religion was false; and (2) although he had positive references to democracy, he clearly displayed a superficial view of it and an unending habit of distorting the basic philosophic doctrines of America's Founding Fathers.

Among the men Grace came to know were four friends who were on the staff of the Communist newspaper, *The Daily Worker.*

None of them seemed settled in mind as to whom to follow and, as the growing circle met to talk and play and argue, there seemed but one agreed position; that was to shy away from any discussion of the divisions so apparent within the Communist Party itself.

A year before she married David, one of the four, some of the enthusiastic Party members recognized her great literary ability and proposed that the magazine give Grace a vacation so that she might return to North Carolina and begin her first novel. Apparently she had long since graduated from the subscription department and was receiving commendation for her own articles and other contributions to the magazine. The time away from New York proved a great boon and a solid delight. She based her story on an actual and severe strike in the textile mills in one section of her state, and she used Lenin's call for "a chance for all to enjoy the good things in life" as her theme song. The story fairly flowed, and when she sent the half-finished book to a publisher, she had a contract within three days which led to its publication and to Grace's fame as a left-wing writer. Advance money allowed her to resign her office job altogether in order to finish the book, and when it was published the reviews were universally enthusiastic. In fact, before this book had fully run its course it became a successful Broadway show and Grace had only to walk through the New York theatre district to see her name in electric lights.

A bright future opened up as the Communist Party leadership accepted the first book as a real proletarian novel. But, as with all people who embrace materialism, a hardening of her spirit and a queer sense of personal deterioration proceeded apace. More and more she was expected to do less original thinking and let the Party think for her.

A second novel appeared, but all was not going well at home. Not that Grace and her husband were not enjoying their fame and their friends and each other. But on any serious subject the husband championed reason, and Grace's constant attempts to convince him that there must be a spirit in man, that there must be a God, had a backlash effect that continuously undermined their relationship.

There came a time when Grace's husband spent less and less of his life on Third Avenue, and then came a period when he would go off for days on end and not even be heard from.

In the spring of 1941 the couple decided to separate. Lonely and bereft, Grace went on living in the Third Avenue flat alone. Her income hardly covered food and rent, but the greater hardship consisted in her isolation and sense of confusion about her purpose and direction in life. She had come to believe deeply in Something, but how this belief could be expressed or how it might enliven her isolated existence she could not imagine. There seemed to be no one with whom she could now talk. She slept fitfully and would often wake up suddenly with a sensation of horror at the *nothingness* both within and without.

One morning about three o'clock she awoke with the feeling that her desolation had reached its bitterest depths. She turned on the light for a moment, only to be reminded of the utter loneliness of her condition. Switching the connection off again, she sat there on her bed bound in grief. Her pride and self-sufficiency shattered, at last she simply stretched up her arms in the darkness and cried, "O God, if there be a God, please help me." And almost before she had finished speaking the miracle happened. A deep peace and quiet came upon her and she soon felt it all around her in the empty room. She was not alone anymore. The most loving Spirit, more loving than any earthly father or mother, surrounded her, and for the first time in ages she went easily back to sleep and awoke rested and refreshed.

After a meager breakfast she reached for some blank sheets of paper and began to write. It was her daily work. But it would not "go." She tried again and again, feeling a longing to describe the experience of the night before, but nothing came. Finally she took a piece of note paper and wrote a letter to her sister, who she knew had faith, telling her that her husband and she had parted and asking what she should do to let God help her. Then she went out to post the letter.

Beyond the post office she turned down Fourth Avenue and there, within a block or two, she noticed a large cross hanging over the steps of an old brownstone church. As she approached this building she saw to her joy that the entrance was open. Inside, in the cool, darker atmosphere, she slipped into a pew and knelt down. Then, there it came again, that gentle sense of an all-embracing love that seemed to answer her deepest need. She does not remember how long she knelt there, but at last, looking up, she saw a lighted altar with a white, marble figure of Jesus Christ standing in the central niche above it. Delighted, she walked down the long center aisle toward the chancel, and as she did so she noticed another lighted area in the front of the church and a brown, paneled door. On the steps before the altar she knelt again and then, rising, felt strangely drawn toward the door. It opened easily and she stood in the attractive, lighted lobby of the adjoining building, Calvary House. Two or three other people moved past as she timidly looked this way and that until she saw a small reading room. This was Grace's dish of tea, and she entered to look at the displays of books and magazines. She was especially glad to find an elderly woman in charge, a gracious person with whom she felt she could talk. Beginning with questions about the literature, she found herself going on and on, first slowly and then more rapidly, describing her experience of the night before.

"Come on. Let's sit down," said Elsie Bowers, the head of the book room, and the two women settled into a conversation which made clear many of the convictions Grace had come to privately on her own. In fellowship together the two women explored what it might mean to find a living faith and how to go about a new way of life.

After an hour or so, Elsie had a suggestion. (She was a dear old gal, rather deaf but with a twinkle in her eye.) She got up smiling and beckoned to Grace. "Come on," she said, "we're going straight back into that old church and have some spoken prayer together."

And that's just what happened. In the side chapel Grace knelt and prayed, pouring her heart out in intercession and thanksgiving, and then Elsie prayed, and when it was all over something more, something quite specific, had taken place. Grace felt launched on a new and God-centered path, with several very clear leadings as to the next steps she should take personally. One of them was to get clear of her Third Avenue quarters. Another was to start writing again, no longer in the vein of materialistic atheism but rather to express those fuller, freer truths that underlie and comprise the Christian faith.

Then at small fellowship groups, as well as at services of Holy Communion, Grace continued to sense God's presence and direction. Week by week, as she heard people speak openly about a living God who was revealed to them especially in His Son, "the living Christ," spiritual assurance deepened within her. At the same time she began to read the Bible again and found it like a new book. In the story of the prodigal son she discovered a parallel to her own experience. As with the prodigal so with her: she had experienced a conviction of sin and returned to her Father. She realized that God had been able to come to her that night alone because she had at last abandoned her proud ego.

Quite quickly thereafter she found a part-time secretarial job which covered her basic expenses, and a few months later she moved into a quiet room right in Calvary House. Then her typewriter began to click again, and week by week she created a moving, faith-filled novel, eventually published under the title *Full Circle*. In this largely autobiographical story, she told about the emergence in the South of a nucleus of faith-motivated and faith-creating people who discovered and lived out Christian answers to difficult labor problems characteristic of a large section of America.

Grace likewise participated in our expanding publishing work, contributing articles to *The Evangel* and helping the editors with many of their rewrites. She also became the secretary of a clergy school for young ministers who wanted a year of internship, a brainchild of the rector that was started by Sam Shoemaker with the help of Canon Quintin Warner of London, Ontario, and Ernest Churchill, a priest in the Diocese of New York.

One day, in casually looking over the secondhand books in a shop on Fourth Avenue, Grace found a copy of the Declaration of Independence in a child's history book. She bought the book and began to review it and then other great documents upon which the United States of America was founded. She shared her discoveries with her new spiritual family and sincerely felt the documents contained the most important and certainly the most beautiful words she had ever read.

"All men are created equal and are endowed by their Creator with certain inalienable rights."

She rejoiced in a new-found sense of personal and civic equality and her spirit became contagious, with the result that the fellowship at Calvary experienced a surge of patriotism. Even more important was Grace's reminder to us that the reality of men's equality derives from the fact that we are all children of the same Father.

Grace called our special attention to words from Washington's Farewell address:

"Of all the dispositions and habits which lead to political prosperity, religion and morality are indispensable supports. In vain would that man claim the tribute of patriotism, who would labor to subvert these great pillars of human happiness, these firmest props of the duties of man and citizens . . . and let us with caution indulge the supposition that morality can be maintained without religion. . . . Reason and experience both forbid us to expect that national morality can prevail in exclusion of religious principle."

*   *   *

While still living at Calvary House, Grace Lumpkin was eventually engaged to act as a proofreader in a small printing plant in Mt. Vernon, New York. Five others made up the staff: the plant foreman, the pressman, two linotypers, and a "bank boy."

All brought their lunches and ate together in one corner of the huge plant that was big enough to house several airplanes. Lunch was the time they talked.

Pete, the foreman, dominated the conversation. He was an excellent worker, but somewhere along the way he had got off the track in his thinking. He spoke bitterly about "the rich" and pointed out all the faults of our country. While not a Communist, he talked their line.

Luncheons were not very pleasant because not only did Pete try to tear down all the values which Grace had learned were important, but the others sided with him. The talk was rough. The plant, with its machines, the dirt, the low level of conversation, and the prison-like supervision, seemed an ugly place.

It had become Grace's practice to pray about certain people and problems; so each morning before work she stopped in at Calvary church and concentrated on the situation in the shop. This became a daily habit.

One day at lunch Pete was in a particularly propagandizing mood. "Human beings are nothing but a higher form of animal," he said. "There's no right or wrong. Everything is relative. It's the churches that stir up the trouble."

"Not the churches, Peter," Grace spoke out suddenly, "but you and I, because we have denied God."

"What do you know about it?"

"I know because I was with the Communist Party for ten years," Grace answered.

The others stared at her in amazement, perhaps wondering how a woman like her could ever have become so involved.

"I used to preach all those things you have been saying," she went on. "I sneered at God and the church. I told lies, cheated, and approved of stealing and murder because I believed the end justified the means. In spirit I was a traitor to my country. We talked a lot about the equal rights of man, but it was only when I accidentally read our own Declaration of Independence that I understood we have no rights and no equality except as we believe in God."

"My wife and I were married in a church," contributed one of the other men lamely.

Peter didn't say another word then, but Grace knew he was angry. Later he called her into the shop, where she found him holding a sheaf of proofs in his hand. In a rasping voice, aimed to be heard by all, he pointed out every minor mistake Grace had made in the last week. She didn't attempt to justify them because she knew the work was basically sound, that his rage had nothing to do with the proofs. Yet it was a humiliating experience. Grace walked to her desk fighting back tears of anger. Furious, she wanted to triumph over Peter, to humiliate him as he had humiliated her. Then she remembered her recent vow to pray over upsets at the very moment they occurred.

"Thy will be done in this place and in my heart," she whispered fervently. At first she couldn't possibly mean it. She had to say it over and over again until peace came to her—peace and confidence and love.

From then on, there were fireworks almost daily during their lunches. Grace was determined to answer all false statements with the truth as she knew it, and she was armed with the facts about Communism. But only through prayer was she able to do this without personal animosity.

Pete and the others, like so many who had been disappointed in life, were the obvious, easy marks for the Communist line. Several times Grace stressed the fact that Communism's emphasis on materialism as a way of life made its followers virtual slaves to their leaders. It had done so to her until she transferred her loyalty to another kind of leader, Christ, who never broke a promise, who never let anyone down, and who makes man free.

For months they tried to shake her stand. She would sit there eating her lunch or knitting, and as she did so she prayed for each one in turn, as well as for herself—that she could be honest, sincere, and understanding.

One noon Pete said: "Why do you say Communists are against religion? They let the churches alone in Russia."

"While still with the Party," Grace answered, "I was told by firsthand observers how religion was fought there. Really religious people get no benefits. They are last when it comes to ration cards, last to get essentials, first to be oppressed. Just as it was in Nazi Germany. These are facts. Communist children are expected to tell the secret police if their parents worship God."

"Well, what makes you think America is so wonderful?" Pete came back. "That book we are printing points out that all newspapers in this country are controlled by the rich, that seventy-five percent of the news is lies. Russian papers tell the truth."

"You are misquoting that book."

He insisted that he was not.

After lunch Grace found the galleys and brought them down to Pete. "Read this galley," she said.

Reluctantly he did. The galley stated that some seventy-five percent of Americans are misinformed on foreign affairs through poor newspaper reporting, not that seventy-five percent of the newspapers print lies.

When Pete finished reading, his face was red. "Go back to your desk," he yelled. He had a heavy file in his hand and he flung it clear across the room against the wall.

Grace left, trembling. An urge to try and rouse the others to mutiny welled up. She knew they, too, resented Pete's behavior. And then she sickened at what she had been thinking. She was not there to have a personal fight with Pete. It must be God's will and God's victory, not hers.

Suddenly it struck her that she must go and say something to Pete *at that moment.*

Pete was at one of the linotype machines with his back to her. She hadn't adequate words, so she walked up to him and touched him lightly on the shoulder. When he turned around dourly, she smiled, at the same time praying hard. The tense muscles around his face relaxed and he smiled back. He stuck out his hand. Grace shook it, then went to her desk.

More months passed and Grace began to notice a definite

change in the plant and in Pete. Nothing startling. They still argued at lunch, but without bitterness.

One morning Grace said: "You know, Pete, you and I both have had a lot of disappointments in our lives."

His nod was friendly. Then he told her how he had married young and had never been able to complete his education. He had never owned his own home. Grace told him how often she gave her disappointments to God.

Shortly afterward Pete said, with an air he tried to make casual, "Amazing coincidence, but I went to church with my family last Sunday and the minister preached about giving your disappointments to God. How do you figure that?"

Although he had gone to church, Grace could see that Pete was ashamed to have the other men know. Even to say the word "church" during lunch had always produced a dead silence or ridicule. How could he acknowledge that he had gone back on all those things he had said?

One morning during her prayers Grace asked God to show her how to get Pete to do this without losing face. That day at lunch Pete began to tell about a Sunday excursion he had taken with his wife and kids. "Was that after church?" Grace slipped in.

"That's right," Pete said without blinking, and finished his story.

After that, religion often came naturally into the conversation. One man who had been most profane in his swearing and had backed Pete most emphatically, spoke one day of church in a very familiar manner. A younger man said "What do you know about it, Bill? You never go to church."

"What the hell!" Bill retorted. "What do you mean I don't go to church! I was in church last Sunday." They all laughed.

The biggest thrill came shortly after. Pete's kids were baptized—and so was Pete. He became an active member of his church, vividly punctuating his conversation with the Bible phrase "with God all things are possible!"

One day Pete said: "Will you pray for me today? I am going to meet some lawyers to talk over buying a house."

Would she? She didn't tell him that for weeks she had been praying that God would make this possible. She was as happy as Pete when he came back and said it was all arranged.

Soon the whole shop was a different place. But Grace knew that it wouldn't stay that way if she let up, that people are always changing one way or the other and that if the change isn't a steady change for the better, it will be for the worse. As she put it, she had learned to *keep God as foreman,* and all things will work together for good.

13/
A Chicago Lawyer Sees Sam

*I*n the early fifties, at a time when national attention was focusing on the alarming increase in American divorces, 33 North La Salle Street, Chicago, used to be a highly satisfactory place for an Illinois plaintiff to go for action. The firm of Cantwell and Cantwell had their law offices there and L. Yager Cantwell, a thirty-three-year-old bachelor and junior partner, had already become a seasoned practitioner of the exacting art of courtroom procedure. Wary of institutional Christianity and suspicious of clergymen, he nevertheless possessed a private brand of sturdy Christian faith. Also, rather well-concealed behind his law practice lay a creative interest in poetry. Unknown to most, he had created dozens of short lyrics of his own.

One morning our poetic attorney woke up with the startling conviction that his literary efforts might well be as marketable as his legal services. Thus it came about that, at the end of a ten-day legal trip to New York City, he arranged an afternoon hour with an editor of E. P. Dutton & Company. He also had a dinner date coming up with a statuesque blonde model, after which he planned to take a late nonstop flight back to O'Hare.

The business conference took place at 300 Park Avenue South where Louise Townsend Nicholl had her editorial office. He had never seen Miss Nicholl and she in turn knew nothing whatever about him beyond a few samples of his poetry. For forty minutes the two talked business most pleasantly. Then the editor paused a moment as if in deep thought, looked intently at the lawyer and asked, "Do you know Sam?"

A bit startled at this apparently irrelevant question Yager asked, "Sam who?"

"Sam Shoemaker."

"No-o-o. Why?"

"Oh, I just thought you might. You know nothing about him at all?"

"Well, I'm not sure," said Yager, fencing. "The name is vaguely familiar. Should I know him?"

"He's written quite a number of books. I thought maybe you'd read one."

"No, I'm afraid not. What kind of stuff does he write?"

"Some of his books are over there on the shelf."

As a matter of pure courtesy, the lawyer walked to the bookcase in question, looked at the titles of the Shoemaker books, came back, sat down, and said nothing. The two conferees at once resumed their business discussion, but after a few more minutes, Miss Nicholl again abruptly remarked: "You know, you really should meet Sam."

"Well, I'm sure I'd like to." Cantwell spoke politely but, inwardly annoyed, he returned immediately to the crucial publishing details under discussion.

Five more minutes on business and then, to his utter astonishment, he heard Miss Nicholl say, "Would you meet Sam if I made an appointment?"

Not trusting himself to say a word, the lawyer stared. Running through his mind was, *What in hell has Sam Shoemaker got to do with what we're talking about! If this gal really wants me to meet her man Sam, she sure has missed the bus.*

By now it was clear that "Sam" was a clergyman. Unfortunately, though an ardent believer, Cantwell's two decades of latent resentment against "churchianity" were bubbling onto the floor of his consciousness. What came out next was short and curt and his body language gave him away. He could conceive of nothing rational, logical, or even supplementary which might justify a meeting with Sam Shoemaker, and for once he decided to give up all attempts at concealing his feelings.

Again Miss Nicholl wisely dropped the subject.

About 4:30 P.M., when Cantwell started to say goodbye, Louise Nicholl was also on her feet. "Will you at least do me a favor?" she asked abruptly.

"Well, yes. Of course. If I can, sure."

"Then please simply stay quiet with me here for two minutes. Together let's see if you *should* see Sam."

Suddenly Yager Cantwell understood. *Stay quiet? Nonsense! Here was a woman working for the same boss he was trying to work for, and what she wanted was for him to pray with her.*

"Of course I will," he replied. And he sat down and covered his eyes.

Once before he had had a strikingly visual answer to prayer. Now for a second time, to his intense surprise, he had another, one that flashed across his inward consciousness like the bright words of a huge neon sign. The words were simply "see Sam." In perhaps forty-five seconds, and beyond all reasonable doubt, here came his answer, directly upon asking, and directly counter to his own rational opinions. God at least had lost no time.

There was a pause and as Miss Nicholl and he shyly looked up at each other, Yager smiled. "You're right," he said. "I *should* see Sam."

The editor was already reaching for her 'phone. She dialed a number. "Busy. We'll wait a moment." Then she got through. The lawyer could tell by listening to her end of the conversation that she was talking with another woman. "Sam can't be disturbed," she reported with a hand over the mouthpiece. "His secretary says he's left explicit instructions. He's counseling a young married couple."

"Here," said Yager impulsively, "let me talk." He reached across the desk. "How long will the counseling last?" he asked. "It's hard to tell," answered the sympathetic voice of Sam's secretary. She sounded as frustrated as Miss Nicholl, but she did have a suggestion. "If you're with Miss Nicholl, you're only a block and a half from Gramercy Park. Why don't you walk over and wait until Mr. Shoemaker is free?" The lawyer agreed to do just that.

Miss Nicholl now appeared to be someone who had been especially prepared to speak to his spiritual condition, and, smiling, she seemed to know exactly what to say. She put it in a godly but down-to-earth way. "In case you should miss Sam, or in case he's still tied up, leave a message. He should know the one simple fact that you and I stayed quiet here together for two minutes and prayed. Then I'm sure he'll see you somehow. And God bless you. I'll be waiting to hear what God had in mind for you two!"

Out on the avenue Yager saw the squat, brown pile of a church; it sat almost diagonally opposite. He crossed and walked past it, turning into Twenty-first Street. Yep, there was Calvary House all right.

Inside, the girl at the switchboard seemed to be expecting him. "Make yourself at home." She pointed to the lobby. "I'm afraid you'll have to wait."

Yager knew how to wait. He sat down recalling people who over the years had waited for him in Chicago. It was maybe 4:45. The receptionist had a suggestion: "Why don't you go up to the second floor? Mr. Shoemaker's secretary is still there."

Good idea. The lawyer took the elevator to the second floor, and sure enough, from across a charming but dimly lighted room he heard a typewriter.

"I'm Yager Cantwell," he announced at the door of an inner office.

"Oh!" gasped the same voice he had heard earlier over Miss Nicholl's telephone. "You scared me. I'm Marian and I'm afraid I'm about to go home. It looks as if you're plain out of luck. Mr. Shoemaker is still busy and I guess he won't be able to see you tonight after all."

"H-m-m-m. Yeah."

"Oh, I'm so sorry." Marian sighed and added, "I honestly don't know what to say. If you could stay over and telephone him in the morning, that is, if you *must* see him personally. Perhaps the two of you could make some arrangement. He's got a terrible day to-morrow, too. He's really a pretty busy man."

"H-m-m-m," repeated the lawyer. "Well, thanks, and please don't let me keep you. I'll just sit outside here awhile longer."

Back at his hotel Yager called the airline and rescheduled his flight for Thursday afternoon. It all seemed a bit confusing, but two sure facts stood out: he was to "see Sam" and, by George, he could and would do it. The dinner date was cancelled and, in due course, he introduced himself to Sam Shoemaker over the 'phone on Thursday morning about 9:15. The latter's appointment book was solid for the day.

CANTWELL: "Well, you've got to eat. How about lunch?"

SHOEMAKER: "Can't possibly do it. There's a man here from out of town."

CANTWELL: "Dinner?"

SHOEMAKER: "No. Sorry. I'm tied up from five o'clock on, far into the evening. We have an open meeting going this Thursday night."

CANTWELL: "Well, look, I'm a trial lawyer. Have to be in Chicago tomorrow, no later than 10 A.M., but I know I'm supposed to see you. It doesn't take any brains to obey and in this case I *want* to be obedient. Incidentally, your friend Louise Nicholl told me to say that she and I stayed quiet in her office for two minutes."

SHOEMAKER (with a laugh): "Bless her heart. If Louise said that, I'll see you somehow. I don't know just when. Maybe I can postpone one of my appointments. Call me back, can you? Say in twenty minutes?"

With Yager's return call there came a break in the clouds. The rector had been able to postpone Thursday's luncheon and Yager was now going to "see Sam" at 12:15. Where? In the Gramercy Park Hotel. Yager would be in a dark suit and Sam would be wearing his "dog collar."

Greatly relieved at the thought of not having to cancel another flight, the lawyer relaxed, opened his briefcase, and continued preparation for the next day's trial in Chicago.

Yager arrived at the rendezvous well before noon, and when the maitre d' heard that he was expecting the rector of Calvary Church, he grinned and led him to a convenient table. Sam was also prompt, and it was a matter of minutes before the Chicago lawyer launched into his story. It was only Louise Nicholl's persistence, and the way he himself had felt that God had spoken to him directly, which explained his being in Gramercy Park, not back in Chicago. Sam nodded, consuming his chef's salad as he listened. "It sounds just absurd enough to be right," he commented. "But go back and tell me how you first got started listening to God and feeling that you belonged to Him." The lawyer described an earlier "happening."

As Sam finished his dessert he looked up and said, "You're not going to Chicago this afternoon. You're coming back to Calvary House around four-thirty for what we call a team meeting. We'll have a big crowd, and the truth is I'd like to have you tell this story of yours during the evening program just as you've told it to me. But first you must be at the team. All kinds of people come early to help us get set for the evening. Come anytime after four. You'd better check out of your hotel and bring your bags with you."

Yager was stunned. "Oh, I really can't do that. You don't realize the pressure on a lawyer these days. Besides, I haven't the slightest idea what you mean by a 'team,' nor do I see any purpose in my speaking at a religious meeting." Lamely he added, "I don't even know what a 'team' is all about."

"Then come and see," laughed Shoemaker, rising.

"Wait a minute. At least tell me when things will be over. What time could I hope to get away?"

"About nine-thirty. Quit worrying." Sam laughed again. "You can shoot for any of half a dozen planes and even leave Calvary House before the meeting is over if you have to. I'll be seeing you."

They shook hands and Sam was gone.

Somewhat dazed, Yager sat over his coffee and reviewed the turn of events. Up to the present he had considered faith a strictly private matter. Was he afraid to let his personal experiences come out into the open? He was about to rebel when he recalled his own reference to obedience. In the taxi returning to the hotel he kept weighing the pros and cons; but an hour later he once again called the airline. Then he packed and finally 'phoned the "statuesque blonde" at her office and suggested that she join him at 61 Gramercy Park at 7:30 for a religious meeting. "I'll explain later."

*   *   *

In the room outside Sam's study on the second floor thirty-two people (Yager counted them) were grouped in a kind of oval. They were of various sizes, shapes, and colors: a Negro clergyman from Jamaica; several people from New Zealand, an assorted half-dozen from Canada; and others seemingly from various sections of the United States—not forgetting New York City. The "sparkly" anticipation was pointed up by Sam's laughter and by the encouraging smile of a younger moderator as they went around the circle asking, "Who are you?" "Why are you here?" and "What recent event has happened in your life through the power of God?"

Yager himself became so excited that, during a pause, lest he miss out, he started to talk—mainly about himself. To his surprise the young moderator good-naturedly cut him off and he was further admonished by Sam: "Chisel it to six or seven minutes at the most."

In the middle of his "verbal gush" (Yager's words) the stairway door had opened yet again, this time admitting four college students—so they proved to be —all from Princeton Theological School. Oh, no! thought Yager. Not Princeton Seminary! The three downright prejudices in my life all stand here together personified in four men not yet dry behind the ears—Princetonians, parsons in the making, and Presbyterians. It can't be true! Two of the students said little besides giving their names, deferring to their companions, and in the end it was mysteriously decided, Yager wondered how, that only one fellow, a chap referred to as "the Nipper," would hold forth at the seven-thirty meeting. Yager's deep-seated antagonism against Princeton men began to melt.

The younger moderator checked his wristwatch. "We'll break up in ten minutes," he said, "but do come back to the Great Hall downstairs pronto at seven-thirty. We'll have some singing; but that's not really the point. Try to meet people as they come in. This evening is *yours* and *theirs*—not Sam's and mine; and you'll be surprised at how much can happen both before and after the speaking. If you want to be theological (this to the seminarians), be simple. And don't think the coffee is waiting just for *you*! Put a cup in the hand of someone you've never seen before. If he's an old Calvary parishioner, so much the better. Now who's got something that simply must be said? O.K. Yes. You bet. Now, Sam, who should lead us in a prayer?"

As the team broke up Yager got up and stretched. It had been fun; he felt sorry the meeting was over. In the crowded elevator on the way up to the rector's apartment for supper he found himself reminiscing: *So that . . . that is a team!*

Downstairs again after a stand-up supper, they could scarcely open the elevator door, such was the crush in the previously deserted lobby. From the meeting room Yager could hear the sound of music as he kept scanning the crowd for the arrival of his beautiful guest. She finally appeared, but there was no time for briefing the girl as Yager had hoped to do. They slipped into a couple of chairs just inside the door.

The meeting began, and what a chairman Sam turned out to be! Yager hadn't believed that anyone could keep so good-humored, at least not at a "religious meeting." Then, almost before he realized what was happening, he heard his own name called and he was on his feet, walking to the platform.

His speech, some told him later, was unfocused and rambling—surely not well-organized for a trial lawyer, he thought. But for a sophisticated trial lawyer to talk about listening to God packed a punch, and his remarks were highlighted by a heckler. The heckling was handled rather nonchalantly by Sam. For Yager it was a godsend—the sort of thing he expected almost everytime he went into the courtroom. Tonight it brought home to him how "far out" some of his audience was. He must keep his story simple and personal. As he spoke, Louise Nicholl was by no means forgotten, in fact she was the center of what he said. He returned to his seat proud that he had taken less than ten minutes.

"The Nipper" came next, and to him Yager listened in curious wonder. A "butterfly" swimming champion at Princeton, aiming for the ministry. Incredible! And the fellow had his audience in one mirthful paroxysm after another. Sam picked up the laughter and commented, "'The Nipper' will laugh more people into the Kingdom than all the rest of us together, though we use the best of our labored techniques."

A Jamaican Negro, a minister, told of the social revolution going on on his island, and after him came a New Zealand woman who had been "healed through faith and prayer." Ralston Young, "Red Cap 42," also had a few minutes in which he told a story of God at work in Grand Central Station. But to Yager the most impressive speaker of the evening was a high-school student who gave what the Chicago lawyer claimed "may have been the best speech I have ever heard." As this lad stood up and walked the twenty feet to a place next to Sam, Yager had just enough time to note his sallow, washed-out, somewhat pimply complexion—"his wavy, flaxen hair that looked as if it had been marcelled an hour before"—characteristics that made him as unattractive an adolescent as Yager thought he had ever seen. But when he opened his mouth, all that Yager could assume was that the Holy Spirit Himself must be coming through. "His speech was supernaturally authored," he said later. In five minutes the boy gave the salient facts about his conversion experience and the new-found life which resulted. But the words Yager remembered, and he may have jotted them down, were these: "I don't know about most of you older folks, or even about many of you who are my age, but if you haven't tried life with Jesus Christ, try it! It's great. It's just great."

Sam took five minutes to sum up and then dismissed the crowd with a benediction. Feet shuffled and the hum of conversation filled the room. The blond model turned astonished eyes on her escort. She was expressing complete bewilderment as, taking his arm, they pressed toward the lobby where the group of Princeton students were standing like lurking beasts of prey.

"Look here," one said, "we don't think you should go to Chicago tonight." A large chap politely blocked his way. "You've heard what Sam said about the walls between undergraduate Princeton and the Theological Seminary down there. We're in touch with both undergraduates and "theologs"—some of them blatant agnostics—but they'd listen to you." Another chimed in. "We'll round up a lot of guys tomorrow night, and as a special bonus I believe Sam would come along too. How about it?"

The lawyer sat down heavily on a bench, twisting uncomfortably. "This is impossible! But to convince you I'll try one 'phone call home."

Astonishingly enough, the old words, "Man proposes, God disposes," once more proved their validity. The Chicago call from the Calvary House hallway 'phone went through directly to his father. Before Yager had a chance to say more than his opening "Hello," the words came back, "Oh, Yager. Glad you called. I've been trying to reach you. The opposing trial counsel 'phoned unexpectedly and asked for a continuance from the Friday trial date." Mr. Cantwell senior said he had agreed to this, had called their client, and notified the witnesses not to appear as scheduled. Nothing else required Yager's presence in Chicago. "Stay as long as you like," was the older man's hearty comment. "That is, so long as you get back for the 'M. case' on Wednesday."

Slightly stunned, Yager hung up. Then for the *third* time he cancelled his flight to Chicago.

Friday sparkled in the autumn air. The streets and buildings of New York City looked rather empty and unusually clean. Yager rose late, having stayed up half the night in a restaurant listening to his beautiful companion talk about her faltering beliefs and her doubt that God could be particularly interested in her small business world.

Early in the afternoon Yager and Sam drove to Princeton. The fifty miles sped by as Yager, completely fascinated, listened to Sam's account of a string of stories about undergraduates in several universities who had recently found faith. Just before the car turned off Route 1, Sam pointed out two Gothic towers. "That's Holder Hall," he said. "The taller one over yonder was built as a memorial to Grover Cleveland. Cleveland was a trustee here when he died." The unique university town displayed the peak of October's brightest colors and to Yager its surrounding hills were breathtaking.

True to their word, the seminarians gathered an impressive crowd of undergraduates, upwards of a hundred, and after a word of introduction from Sam, the sophisticated Chicago lawyer let his young audience have his deepest, personal convictions about the Almighty with a rare freedom only gained the day before. When Sam left to drive back to town, Yager was still hard at it; and so he spent the night and had further time to talk with individual students the next day. At last he caught a train back to the city, weary but in a rosy glow. Checking into his hotel, he got Sam on the 'phone in order to fill him in. "The boys responded, Sam," he reported. "Thought I'd never get to bed."

"Wonderful. Wonderful." The rector exclaimed with characteristic joviality. "It all sounds providential. And now I've got a businessman here who wants to hear your story. Will you come on down?"

As Yager packed, Sunday morning, he resisted an urge to call Sam for a last chat. The rector would doubtless be very busy, and just might urge him to stay for church. Finally, however, he asked the hotel switchboard to try Gramercy 5-1216.

A woman answered doubtfully when he asked for Mr. Shoemaker, but after a moment Sam's strong voice came over the wire. "God speed you, old fellow," he said. "But quickly answer me one question, will you? How exactly do you *know* God answered Louise's and your prayers last Wednesday?"

"How do I know? How do I *know?*" repeated Yager. "Well of course a person can be mistaken, be self-deluded, and a dozen other things the psychiatrists talk about. I can only say that I've never been surer of myself—*never*. I'm not discounting self-hypnosis and what they call psychological releases, triggered by deep, unknown emotional needs. No. But in those moments immediately following our prayers I felt the deepest conviction and the clearest direction. That 'see Sam' was neither desired nor convenient." Yager took a deep breath. "That answer was one of the most important events in my life." He paused. "Say, you're a great one to ask a question like that! Before you preach this morning, Sam, I suggest you stop and think about the consequences. It should spice your sermon."

"Good. I'll do just that," Sam agreed. "What's more, one day I'll write it all down. Now before we ring off promise me two things—first, keep in touch with us and, most important, make sure that this time you *do* catch that Chicago plane!"

As he hung up, Yager had a broad grin on his face. He was going home, but Chicago would be different.

On his return home the Chicago lawyer began to put his faith to work—I might say that he "burst into song." As he wrote me shortly, he could see God's Holy Spirit "stab down and cut like a gleaming knife into the jungles of contested litigation, tumble walls of legal technicalities, and ease the demands of cross-examination."

As a man of faith and a romantic, Yager Cantwell had been viewing such events for a long time, but only in a two-dimensional way. He had been a trial lawyer for seven years before he met Sam Shoemaker. After his trip to New York he continued to abide by the rights, standards, rules, and precedents of the American Bar Association, but he seemed to be viewing his professional activities with a fresh, three-dimensional, spiritual appreciation. A quotation from another of these early letters sounded equally lyrical: "The Holy Spirit enters the lives of clients, witnesses, opposing litigants, and at times mellows the most antagonistic and obstreperous lawyers—including myself!"

In the editorial office of *The Evangel* we were impressed by what was happening in Yager Cantwell's law practice; his awareness that something new was being added, and that this freshness came to him as a direct result of his own developing spiritual experience.

The whole *Evangel* family (a network of like-minded readers around the globe) was keen about any reports of the effect of personal evangelism on social conditions, and we were printing too few stories of the *results* of conversion. Christians with the strongest personal faith so often failed to relate such experience to the situations where they spent most of their waking hours—the office, the factory, or the home. Many were self-conscious and needed prodding to apply the radical truths of the New Testament in places where they might run into opposition or be thought queer. Yager Cantwell, we realized, could spur some of these "reluctant missionaries" into action in dealing with social issues, and so I kept urging him to send me his revolutionary discoveries.

One day a bulky envelope arrived from his La Salle Street office in Chicago, enclosing a story so eloquent and compelling that we immediately handed it around at a staff meeting and decided to use it as the lead article in our next issue, which happened to be March 1953. We entitled it "She Wanted a Divorce" and we made the subhead "The Story of a Client Who Did Not Get Her Way." It created great interest and became the first of a new series of similar pieces which focused on how individuals whose faith had become alive might change their office procedures and/or family life. Here is the story in a condensed form:

One evening a young married woman—Yager suggests calling her Dorothy to preserve complete anonymity—brought me a familiar story. Her love for her husband had turned to loathing and she had twice asked him for a divorce. As she rehearsed her grievances there appeared in clear outline the picture of a life which had gone hollow—the center was without motivation. Even caring for her children—she had two, eight and ten—had lost its meaning and she had come to the place where she was merely existing in a kind of desert. Hers was an arid life without love, faith, or hope.

When I could interrupt, I asked her a few questions: What she thought a divorce would solve. What problems it would raise. What effect it would have on the children's personalities and their future.

She insisted that she had thought of all these angles and was putting the children's welfare before all else. They would be happier, she maintained, if they were living with a mother whose home did not resemble "an armed camp."

Then I asked her what she had tried to do to prevent a divorce, and if she had tried to find an answer to the sterility of her own life. Yes indeed, she replied, that was just where the desperation had come in. She had "tried everything, even prayer," but nothing had worked, "except perhaps those prayers." She had wanted to ask me about them. What did I think about prayer?

"Before I answer," I found myself saying, "I'd like to ask you two more questions: Do you think there's any possibility of your husband or you changing so that you can be happy?" "No, people don't change," she replied. "After reaching a certain chronological maturity they're stuck with whatever psychological immaturity they may happen to have; they settle into their respective ruts and live out their lives in loneliness, never really understanding themselves or each other, and raising children they do not understand." Yes, she was sure of it.

I proceeded to my second question: "What do you believe about God?" She didn't know. She had had two "peculiar experiences." Twice when she had prayed she seemed to be relieved. Was it possible that God answered prayer?

At this point I clearly remember pushing back from the table and silently praying myself. Then I felt guided to remind her of the biblical injunctions *against* divorce. As I did this I could see that this made a visible impression upon her.

We talked for about three hours, during which I tried constantly to invoke divine aid. I spoke of changes that had already occurred in the lives of people she knew—dramatic flip-flops from past conduct—unpredictable changes. Then I brought up some of the New Testament miracles. She had always questioned these but agreed with me that, if they had happened, they must always have been performed with prayer. And I told her I had seen other miracles happen today. "God has never stopped intervening in human life," I insisted. "But He is a polite God. He's got to be invited in."

There was a pause. Then, "How do you invite Him in?"

"Through prayer, dedication, and devotion. Prayer *can* do it."

About midnight I took her to her car. She thanked me, drove off, and I didn't hear from her again for nearly seven months. Not a word. But just before Christmas a letter arrived which meant more to me than a $10,000 fee.

It read: "I'm returning the books in the hope that they may help someone else as they did me. . . . Miracles *can* happen, can't they? Perhaps some day I'll have the chance to tell you more about my little private one and thank you as profusely as I should for the impact of that evening last May. I used to wonder why you chose the legal profession. . . . It was a blessing that you did. . . .

"Thank you sounds utterly inadequate, but I've never said it more reverently. God bless you. Dorothy" I wrote right back to my client, thanked her for writing as she had, and told her I must have more details of her side of the story. She was the only person who could furnish these and I asked her to please write again and spell out what had happened to herself and in her home. When she complied, the tale so moved me that I phoned her for permission to use it anonymously in this very space.

Dorothy's Half of the Story

This is I, Dorothy, the client. I had called my attorney in desperation, having lost all hope of saving my marriage. I needed legal help, but I also had a secret motive for seeing him. I admitted to myself that he was the kind of a person with whom I might wish to have a clandestine relationship. I had known him well, and from the time my marriage began to sour I had been daydreaming about him.

When I arrived at his residence I was excited, and in my love-starved condition, as we talked my anticipation increased—that is, until a certain point in the conversation. Then something happened. I can't remember how or what occurred, but there was an exact moment when I felt sure that a clandestine relationship with this man was not for me. Suddenly it was as if tall walls had gone up around him—probably when he referred to the scriptural injunction against divorce.

I left my lawyer in a very thoughtful mood and when I reached home I felt humiliated, completely. Never in my life had I been as angry and as frustrated. I had had a secret purpose in my heart, but at no time had I revealed my desire for an intimate relationship, and I had done nothing nor made any suggestion that he could reject. In that sense I had no business feeling humiliated, but for thirty-six hours I felt lower and more ashamed of myself than at any other time in my whole life.

Looking back on this experience, I wonder if there isn't a close relationship between *humiliation* and *humility*. I had rarely been humbled before, and God was using my tangled circumstances to help me to learn through suffering *and* to prepare me for what lay ahead. There was still little affection between my husband and myself—it took two more months for that—but I was praying more often and the drab, hollow routine at home became tolerable.

Then John and I were invited to a weekend house party at the home of old friends. Their guest room was occupied and John and I took the davenport in the living room. Lights out and quiet for ten minutes, then John spoke: "What are you thinking?" "I'm praying," I replied. After a long pause I heard him ask: "May I pray with you?" And that of course was the start of the big change and of my own private miracle. We prayed together—for each other, for our marriage, for our children—and affection began to be rekindled.

Life at home gradually became more normal and by autumn there wasn't a cloud in John's sky. My own sky remained cloudy but there were bright intervals. As winter came, I realized I, too, was truly happy—unexpectedly, joyfully, with husband and children thriving.

The two of us were now driving ten miles or more every Sunday morning to listen to a clergyman, a "spiritual man" Yager had told us about. We loved being together this way on the first day of the week. Thanks to this "church home," Christmas and New Year's Eve that year were the best and holiest holidays the family had ever enjoyed, and the two months which followed was the happiest period of our whole marriage.

But my story is in two parts. In March came the tragedy which God was preparing me to meet. Early that month John began to have headaches, but because he'd always been strong and healthy we ignored them and he left town on a business trip. A week later he came down with a fever in New Orleans and 'phoned me long distance to get his bed ready and meet his plane.

It was a very, very sick husband who came through the gate at the airport. He hadn't been able to keep a meal down for three days. The doctor ordered immediate hospitalization and X-rays. When John's fever went up to 105 degrees, the doctor diagnosed him as dangerously ill with a brain tumor.

This frightened me terribly but I knew what to do. I was in my own home and I simply got down on my knees and prayed. And then an event took place—so mysterious, shall I say so supernatural?—that I was overwhelmed and knew that I had been uplifted as well as calmed and strengthened. It was incomprehensible, yes, and glorious. It seemed as if God had entered the very room . . . and placed hands on my forehead. And His unforgettable message was this: "Don't worry. I am with you both. Everything will be all right." After a little while I sat on the bed and telephoned John's relatives to come immediately, and then I went off to sleep soundly.

The next day John's condition grew even worse, indicating an operation regardless of his weakness. I was allowed to see him just before he was wheeled off to the operating room. He was still conscious but couldn't talk. I approached his bed along with the doctor and a nurse and, with a prayer in my heart, it seemed that I knew exactly what to say. "John, you remember what happened the last time we prayed together?" He nodded. "Just keep on praying, and everything will be all right, I know. Just keep on praying."

I never saw him again alive. The doctor came five hours later to tell me that he had died on the table after a three-hour fight to save him.

After my prayer the night before, it had never occurred to me that he could die. I had interpreted God's answer to mean that John would live here and now and I had been unconcerned about anything else. Desperately I drove to the church to see my "spiritual man." He listened patiently, gravely, as I poured out my story. Then he suggested that perhaps what had happened might be a blessing—at least for John—and better for all of us. It was better that John had been taken than that he should have continued in this life as an incurable invalid, perhaps in a wheelchair, or with his mind affected and cooped up for years on end in one of the only convalescent homes available to us at the time.

Three days after the funeral I saw the doctor again. After prefacing his remarks with "I don't know whether I should tell you this," he said, "but the surgeon found the brain damage so severe that John would have been at least partially paralyzed, and perhaps incurably crippled mentally forever."

*   *   *

"You see," wrote Yager, "God had intervened. When my client and I had prayed, God was as good as His promise. When invited in He did intervene—even when Dorothy first came to me about a divorce. I believe that He will do the same for anyone who prays as my client did, depending naturally on the nature of his acknowledged needs."

14 /

Corrie ten Boom and Others Knock on the Door

*T*he Sunday Morning Service was over and Calvary House's Great Hall fairly buzzed with conversation as parishioners and their guests visited near the coffee table. People loved the informality of this hour with its chance to meet Sam and Helen Shoemaker and perhaps one or two of the Calvary or *Evangel* "family" from overseas. Visitors felt at home and soon became knowledgeable about group meetings and other events in the local program for the week ahead. Since the Monday men's meeting used a second-floor room, part of which could be seen from the coffee table, it was easy to inform a business or professional man about this group by simply pointing up to the sliding-glass panels of the balcony. Staffers were trained to add a word such as: "Perhaps we could meet up there about 5:15 tomorrow afternoon."

Staying in Calvary House one spring in the mid-forties was an Episcopal chaplain just returned from service with Canadian Forces in Europe. Though honorably discharged, Handley Perkins still wore his uniform and was enjoying the life and discipline of 61 Gramercy Park for a brief period before returning to local parish work in Ontario. He knew his way around, as it were, and helped us on the staff in many ways while participating in various parish activities; and he invariably kept on the lookout for visitors like himself who were new to Calvary Church. On the Sunday in question he had been taking a last glance around the entrance porch before coming in to the coffee hour when he saw a man and a woman still browsing at the book table in a kind of aimless fashion after all but the girls in charge had left. It didn't take him long to discover that the man was Dr. George A. Little of Toronto, an editor who knew Sam Shoemaker and Calvary well. But the sturdy Dutch woman who also stood there was a total stranger. She seemed as lost as anyone could be who was alone in a foreign country, or in the unattractive wilderness which sections of New York inevitably became of a Sunday morning. She was, in fact, Corrie ten Boom.

"When I saw the cross hanging over the entrance, I just came in," she explained in her halting English. "And I am still here," she added with a laugh.

Chaplain Perkins eagerly recommended the hot coffee so near at hand and enlarged upon the fellowship Miss ten Boom could find only a few steps away. Corrie needed no urging, and a few minutes later the three of us were chatting together in the Great Hall. Over the coffee cups Corrie and I made a date for her to come to *The Evangel* office the next morning to talk over various positive possibilities. When our visitor admitted rather reluctantly that her slim resources had about run out, and smilingly described the 10¢ Nedick breakfasts which had become the order of her days, those in the small group around her easily realized the urgency of her plight.

Was ever there anyone with as engaging a sense of humor as our visitor from Holland! But, on the serious side, the news she recounted the next day sounded savage beyond belief. Yes, she said, she had helped countless Jews escape from Hitler. But then her father, her sister, and she had at last been caught and incarcerated under unspeakable conditions in Nazi concentration camps. She told part of the story of their imprisonment—first in Holland and then in Ravensbruck, Germany—all without a trace of self-pity. Sitting quietly in our editorial office, she related the brutal facts of the ten Booms' suffering, even the account of her father's and sister's deaths. She spoke almost unemotionally but with complete and agonizing and deeply moving frankness. The earlier details of life in their old house in Haarlem, where a team of Christians fooled so many of the Germans for so long, made her laugh. She recalled the terror, but mostly she told of the ingenuity and antics of the enlarged family. Even the youngest members had each his vital role in those distant days and agonizing events.*

She explained that besides her witness to the power of the Lord Jesus Christ, she had lectures and a special rehabilitation project to present—a home, "Schapenduinen," already established in Holland for the war-torn and mentally deranged people of her homeland. "A miracle has brought me to America to tell about my experiences with the Lord in the prison camps and to beg gifts from churches and people who are able to help us. . . . But the doors of the offices where I expected to be heard do not open for me," she hesitatingly confessed. "Secretaries ask to see my 'credentials' and, though I am constantly in prayer about it, I do not know where to turn."

We told her of our Calvary family fellowship in New York and we suggested that she meet with a dozen or more of us on the following Thursday night in our apartment home, so that we could pray together about her needs and ask jointly for God's further light on her plans and prospects.

As she was preparing to leave the office, I remembered a somewhat similar experience which Ernest Gordon had had in the Japanese camp in the Kwai Valley and how this story had electrified our magazine readers when we printed it.

"Haven't you some written account of your own prison days?" I asked. "One which we could put into *The Evangel*."

"But yes," Corrie nodded enthusiastically and smiled. Out of her small, black briefcase came a sheaf of papers. "Here you are, here's the whole story," she said. "Use it as you like."

"That's splendid," I said, taking the papers. "But there's one difficulty. We do not have the funds to pay any of our authors. They give us their material and they seem happy simply to know that their stories of what God has done for them will help our readers and other friends who read such tales."

"Goot. Goot." Corrie's face lit up. "What you say makes me *very* happy. I feared Americans thought only of their dollars. Take anything you want and use it, as you say over here, 'for free.' It is all

---

*For later, more complete stories of these experiences, see the book *The Hiding Place* (Guideposts, 1975) and the motion picture of the same title.

yours and my heart is filled with joy that we don't have to waste time talking of money."

When Thursday night came, much to the delight of our three young children, Corrie was among the first to arrive at our flat. She laughingly admitted that the strange word, which to the youngsters described a loud noise, was really her own name: BOOM! To the amusement of all she then encouraged the bedlam which followed, as "BOOM!" after "BOOM!" echoed through our living room. "And do you know, children," she said, "when I come back from Holland next time, I am going to bring you a cardboard windmill just like the ones in my country, which you can make, arms and all, by fitting the pieces of cardboard together."

We felt an unusual depth of fellowship that evening. None of us had suffered the torment and anguish our honored guest had experienced, and few in the circle had a story comparable to Corrie's account of Jesus' adequacy in man's extremity. But comparisons paled before our joy in experiencing together the presence of God and the breeze of His Holy Spirit. As to the matter of Corrie's "credentials," Helen Shoemaker summed up what all of us felt when she asserted, somewhat impatiently, "Credentials? *Credentials*? Why this woman is her *own* credential!"

Together we thought of a dozen doors that would most gladly open to Corrie so that she might tell American Christians of the special needs of her countrymen and affirm her message, "Jesus is victor." We took care of a few details regarding Corrie's continuing hospitality in New York and, as she herself felt drawn to meet our Norwegian friend, Abraham Vereide, in Washington, D.C., we arranged for this to happen. As she makes clear in a recent book, *A Tramp for God,* from that evening forward she found an overabundance of places where friends welcomed her and even pleaded for her witness and her help, and in various homes and churches she received answers to her urgent financial needs back home.

One instance characteristic of further blessings Corrie experienced before she left on that first visit happened in New York. She asked Grace Lumpkin, one of the staff, to guide her to a certain address in a downtown area. "God has a typewriter for me there," she assured Grace confidently.

Knowing that every cent she could find was going to her work back in Holland, Grace asked "Have you money for the typewriter?"

"No," she answered almost impatiently, in her still rather awkward English, "but God has promised."

Grace suddenly realized the amazing depth of Corrie's trust in God. "You have great faith."

"Oh, no," Corrie protested. "Not great faith, but faith in a great God."

They started off, and over the noise of the subway Corrie explained that a friend in Holland had given her the address of a typewriter company in New York and assured her that the owners were people who believed in God.

They found the place easily and after reaching the proper floor Corrie disappeared into an office, leaving Grace with the receptionist—somewhat skeptical and most anxious that our visitor would not be disappointed.

No one knows what was said between Cornelia ten Boom and the company official with whom she talked, but when she and Grace left to return uptown, Corrie cheerily reported that she had a new typewriter and one for which she had paid nothing! Her face was beaming. "See," she said in her charming English. "How goot is our Gott! He always keeps His promises."

As we separated after Corrie's first visit to the States, none of us had a doubt but that "Jesus is Victor." What we did not realize was that her basic message was under the grace of God; she would become one of the great evangelists of our time. In Bermuda, in 1976, at the fifteenth anniversary of the founding of "Willowbank," the Christian guesthouse, she spoke several times at meetings and with friends, using as a punchline these compelling words: "After you have experienced the worst, if you know the Lord, the best always remains—and the *very* best is yet to be."

In the Elevator

One Sunday, on entering church late, I tagged after the choir as they marched down the center aisle singing the opening hymn, then quickly slipped into a rear pew. Turning toward me, a handsome, matronly woman with white hair shared her hymn book. She was the pew's only other occupant, and as I saw the way she referred frequently to her leaflet, I realized that she was a visitor, doubtless the member of another denomination.

At the end of one of Sam's moving twenty-minute sermons, she smiled at me approvingly as much as to say, "I expected just that kind of a talk." When the service finished a few minutes later I introduced myself as a member of the staff and added a word of welcome.

"I'm Ruth Moulton," she replied. "I take *The Evangel*, and you and I have corresponded about a prayer group I started at the school where I have been head mistress." In answer to a question she went on, "Well, I've just retired, so I shan't be going back to the school. I have a son working in New York so I'm thinking of trying one of your hotels—perhaps one near Calvary House if I can find a room which isn't too expensive."

I told her about The Parkside Hotel, which at the time was patronized by many Calvary friends, and I urged her to come into the coffee hour and meet a few of the congregation.

Bertha Elliott was pouring that day, and as we stood talking she not only described further the hotel situation but added, "If you do come to live near us, you must visit the *Evangel* office. We have a tea in Irving's office every Thursday, but I'm looking right now for some volunteers to help us with the filing in the business office."

Ruth Moulton was a quick mover and within a week she was living at The Parkside and spending her mornings at a desk in Bertha's office. She had a most outgoing personality and made friends fast. Almost every Thursday she would turn up for tea, and she usually had a story to tell about her attempts "to be redemptive in every situation."

One Thursday, as she came in, she whispered, "I've got a special word for you this afternoon." A few minutes later we heard her story:

Every afternoon I go uptown to see an old friend who, I discovered soon after settling in New York, is in the hospital. Last Monday as I stepped from the lobby into one of the elevators my heart was light. My friend was much improved and I looked forward to another stimulating talk with her. The elevator operator smiled at me, sealing my standing as "a regular" among visitors. But my heart sank suddenly when I noticed two others already in the elevator, a nurse and a young man. She carried his coat; and, because the elevator had come up one floor before stopping for me, I knew he must be a clinic patient who was being admitted.

Just as the elevator doors closed on the four of us, the young man cringed in pain. The nurse turned to the operator and tensely ordered: "Take us right up to the operating floor!" As she turned back to her patient, the boy looked at me full face and said in an agonizing voice: "Lady, can you pray? I'm scared. This has all happened so fast."

I grasped his outstretched hands, my mind turned toward God, my thoughts racing. "Our Heavenly Father," I prayed in a voice that was amazingly calm, "come close to this boy. Be with him; give him courage; take away his fear. Stay with him, constantly; through Jesus Christ, Our Lord."

Then, a moment later, just before we reached the top floor, I suggested: "You pray now." When he shook his head that he couldn't, I urged him, "Just say, 'Our Father.' You know that."

"I couldn't get through it," he answered weakly.

The elevator stopped, but the operator made no move to open the door. The nurse anxiously tried to do it herself. I had one more thought. I said: "Say just some little prayer your mother taught you."

Still grasping my hands, he started: "Now I lay me down to sleep. I pray the Lord my soul to keep. If I should die before I wake . . . He paused for a moment and then repeated: "If I should die before I wake, I pray the Lord my soul to take—and this I ask for Jesus' sake."

The elevator doors opened. His hands relaxed. The nurse took his arm and helped him walk slowly, painfully, toward the operating rooms.

I was so deeply touched that, after visiting my friend, I went home and prayed for that boy the rest of the afternoon.

While I was sitting in my friend's room at the hospital the following day, I looked up and saw, standing in the open door, the nurse of the day before. She beckoned me to her.

As we strolled down the long hall, she said: "You know that nurses are not allowed to tell what goes on in hospitals. But I have special permission to tell you this. Just before he went under ether, that boy said, 'Please tell the lady in the elevator that I am not scared now, and I think I feel God close to me.'"

"Oh, how wonderful!" I exclaimed. "How is he? When can I see him?"

To which she replied: "Everything was done, but he died during the operation."

The Doctor and His Wife

The editor of a small magazine has a special day periodically which he both loves and fears. His articles are written, the editorial and the news items have been composed, proofreading has been completed, and the masterpiece is to be "put to bed." He enjoys a happy latitude in arranging and preparing his "dummy" for the printer, and his artistic skill and past experience combine to give him a keen relish for this concluding step toward which the work of the past weeks has been moving him. He has scarcely any need but for time. Interruptions must be avoided at all costs.

Such a day was proceeding cheerily. The morning saw the solution of the usual problems of lack of space and a good half of the galley proofs had been carefully cut and pasted in position when, in the cool of the afternoon, with another twenty pages to go, that occasionally provoking instrument, the telephone, broke the quiet with a series of particularly loud, shrill rings.

"The Stephens of Toronto are in the front hall asking for you," said Winnie apologetically.

"Oh! All right," I answered wearily. "I'll be down."

Putting a small dictionary on the dummy, and pushing the proofs aside, I headed for the elevator. But then in the descending car came the chance to catch my breath and ask for a renewal of the Spirit. Believe me I needed it. Reaching the ground floor I found a most attractive couple and gave them a warm welcome.

"Dr. Steve" had a face the shape of a full moon. His dark, lovely wife stood beside him; both seemed slightly embarrassed. "We're in New York on one of our spring holidays," the doctor said, "and just came down to pay you a passing call, as I had promised one of my patients to see you. But we really haven't a moment and we certainly don't want to bother you."

"Oh, do come upstairs for a few minutes," I said. "Now that you're here I'd like you at least to see our magazine office."

They reluctantly condescended and we took the elevator to the fourth floor. Back in the editorial sanctum I did my ineffective best, but a sense of uneasiness took possession of us. I pointed to the park, which could be seen from one window, and to the church, visible from another. But our guests couldn't have been less interested and even declined to sit down for more than a moment or two.

"Thanks," the doctor said. "You're busy and we're leaving for home tomorrow. Just tell Dr. Shoemaker we stopped by because of friends up north, and we'll look forward to meeting all of you some other time."

I slipped in a word or two about the work and outreach of our magazine to friends in his part of Canada, but got not a spark in return.

"Well," I stammered, "I *am* busy. Still it would be good to have an unhurried talk. Perhaps you could come to our apartment to-night for a cup of coffee. We live just a few blocks away."

Mrs. Stephens looked interested at this but made no comment and the doctor simply countered hastily, saying, "No, no. We're sorry but it's the last night of our visit and we're all set for a show."

Now I've always been a rather shy old bird and rarely think of asking questions about the state of people's souls, but at that moment I had a strange, strong impulse to raise a prayer for these two before they left, and almost involuntarily I found myself putting a hand on the doctor's shoulder. "Let's just ask God to bless us all," I said.

It seemed a long minute or two, that prayer. Secretly Mrs. Stephens had brought with her a problem regarding family relations, and as we prayed God was at work. Then the unexpected happened. As we opened our eyes, the doctor and I saw a stream of tears flowing down his wife's face.

"Steve," she said with a catch in her throat, "I do feel the need of talking with this man about our home situation. Let's skip the show and accept Mr. Harris's suggestion of that cup of coffee."

Obviously annoyed, the doctor felt himself trapped. "Well," he said glumly, "suppose I call you a bit later. Give me your number and we'll see how things go."

At home, over the apple pie, we got his 'phone call. "That you?" asked Dr. Stephens, his voice still expressing irritation. "My wife does seem a bit upset. Tell you what. We'll drop in for half an hour or so. We'll let the show go and take in a late movie."

Shortly after eight, the buzzer on the apartment door announced the Stephens' arrival. Introductions over and our children off to bed, my wife and I drew up chairs for them around the fireplace. Steve had no intention of letting his family problems come out into the limelight, but it proved a great evening. We found we had all sorts of things in common, and at last we did talk about the irritations and rivalries that keep those in the same family apart. I had a chance to describe a new, weekly men's meeting at Calvary Church, and the way a period of silence so often brought insight and freedom and even healing in such a group.

"Sounds so simple," the doctor commented, and after another story or two, he repeated, "All they do is to talk honestly about what's bothering them, and pray. How simple it is!"

At this I felt compelled to bring things to a head. "It interests you, doctor, and as you say it *is* simple. Why, instead of just talking about it, don't we try a spot of prayer here and now, and ask for light on your own situation?"

"Wait. Wait a minute!" The doctor drew back. "It's fine for you to pray, but I've never prayed aloud in my whole life."

"But there's always a time and a place to begin," I countered. "My wife's a good pray-er. She'll start us off. Then if you want to be quiet, and pass, that's quite all right."

Down went our heads and Julie bravely took the ball. She thanked the Lord for our new-found friends and asked His blessing on us all.

It was Steve's turn, and not a word—only one of those awful pauses whose minutes seem like hours. No one in the circle stirred, and I just held my breath. Then suddenly the silence was broken as the doctor's deep voice boomed out emotionally. "O God, here I am. If You want me, take me. But if You want me, take me *now*. And if you take me, take my wife, my children, my home, my money, and my talents whatever they are. God, take everything I have, but do it right now. Amen."

Quite a prayer! He had given away his life and he sat, dripping wet and exhausted. By this time his wife was weeping again and her muffled, "Thank you, thank you, Lord," broke up that prayer group on the spot. She looked up, half laughing, "I'm not crying now in distress," she explained, "but for joy. That's the very first time in all our married life I've ever heard my husband pray. It's wonderful."

Julie and I agreed. "You better go along to the kitchen," the former suggested, "and brew us all a pot of strong, Canadian-made tea."

Shows and movies now seemed forgotten as we talked and talked about a new quality of life. "Now that the cork has come out," I suggested, "you won't have to keep things bottled up any more."

The tea about took the roof off our mouths but the new spirit of joy and freedom filled the room. "You know," said the doctor, "in those two minutes of prayer, I discovered the secret of life. By simply turning to God we can be free of all the terrible things we keep carrying around inside us and that make for our anxieties and fears and tensions and neuroses. The miracle is performed through prayer—by participation in prayer."

What a release! What a promise of good things to come! When that couple left in the early hours of the morning, it was as if we had known one another for years. At breakfast they 'phoned from the airport. "We're off," the doctor shouted, "but boy, oh boy, how excited we are, especially in knowing that everything at home will be on a different basis. Yeah, we talked another hour at the hotel, and Lillian had to have *her* prayer. Now we're both really full of beans about the future. We'll be in touch."

We *were* in touch, week by week, and letter by letter, and in His own way God multiplied what He started in our meeting wherever that re-made doctor and his wife went. And talk about a new practice! Here's just one of the dozens and dozens of stories Steve sent us in his letters in the days that followed:

"Last Saturday night I was preparing to have a nice quiet evening at home when the 'phone rang. A man wanted to know if I would come and see his wife who was 'having hysterics.' I dragged myself to my car and drove over to their beautiful country home. In a spacious bedroom I found the lady weeping, while her husband was trying to console her by getting drunk. I listened to her troubles for thirty minutes and gave her the usual inane advice and some strong sedatives to make her sleep. When I got up to go and shook hands, I felt that I had accomplished exactly nothing. It was then that the woman's eyes filled with tears and she said, 'Oh, doctor, I wish there was something that I could pin my faith to.'

"I had been thinking all along that what this woman needed was just to hand her troubles over to God, as my wife and I had just done. At this point, her husband entered the room again surprising us with a tray and three glasses of whisky on it. I thanked him, took a glass, and sat down on a comfortable chair, 'sighted my gun,' and let go. 'Are you people atheists?' I inquired innocently. They each took a good slug of Scotch and hastened to assure me that they were not. 'Then why not pin your faith in God?' (This caused an expression of slight alarm on both their faces.) 'Don't you ever talk to God about your problems?' I asked.

"The husband turned to his wife. 'Why, come to think of it,' he admitted, 'we haven't said our prayers since we were first married twenty-five years ago!'

"There followed over three hours of down-to-earth talk which carried each of us up to the clouds. The drinks were forgotten. Finally the husband turned to me. 'You haven't told me one thing I didn't know before, but it all sounds different tonight.'

"The breeze of the Spirit, boy, how it worked! I had suggested to them that they make a practice of praying together every day about every single problem that confronted them, and that they let God look after their problems instead of trying to worry their way through on their own. I repeated, 'This is my prescription for you both.'

"That was the end of the hysterics. The next morning I dropped around to see how my patient was. She and her husband were *both* radiant."

15/
Faith at Work Moves Uptown

*I*t was late on a Tuesday evening in October 1955. The 'phone rang sharply in my room at 90 Park. Sleepily, I turned over on the bed, letting the morning *Herald Tribune* slide to the floor, and answered. The voice belonged to the new rector of Calvary Church, the younger man who had succeeded Sam Shoemaker in Gramercy Park.

"Can you see me first thing when you come in tomorrow?"

"Yes, of course," I said. "What's up?"

"I want to talk to you as early as possible. That's all."

I could sleep on this without difficulty, but the timing of the call surprised me, and as I left the club the next morning to meet my friend, I felt even more perplexed. Why this extraordinary summons? At a recent staff meeting we had seemingly met in the usual happy way and begun the planning of fall programs for both the parish work and our special ecumenical activities. Yes, we'd been in full and hearty accord.

Shortly we faced each other across the younger man's desk. He looked excessively grim.

"Two friends of yours were talking with me when I 'phoned you last night," he began. "We had decided that if I am to carry on properly here as rector, despite my previous backing, it will be best that your work, in fact all ecumenical activities should go."

"And *The Evangel* magazine?" I asked.

"Yes, that too."

I felt for the big chair opposite him and sank down rather heavily. After a moment or two I asked, "Have you talked over this amazing proposal with your senior warden?"

"The acting senior warden didn't show up at the vestry meeting last night." Then irrelevantly, "You like that man, don't you?"

"Yes, I certainly do," I said. "And of course he has always backed the magazine and our conference work to the full." There was a pause. "You and your colleagues have always encouraged us to continue *The Evangel,* the group work, and even public evangelistic meetings," I added.

"These must go, too—everything connected with extraparochial activities."

Another pause. "If you haven't talked to your warden," I finally said, "would you mind if I try to get him on the 'phone right now so you can tell him what you've just told me?" And, as he nodded, I leaned over the desk and picked up the 'phone.

"Ken," I said, as the call went through, "here is the rector. He has some extraordinary news for you."

As I listened, I heard the two men set a time when they could get together.

Inwardly, every manner of question ran through my mind. What had happened to turn this ally into an opponent? Had I taken his backing too much for granted? Was he feeling unhappy in his work, or had friends specially close to him persuaded him that evangelism was for the birds and that the rector of a local Episcopal church should not tolerate ecumenical activities in his parish? I detected a new and surprising animosity toward both his predecessor and myself. What could have occasioned it?

Completely baffled, the interview over, I went looking for my colleagues Bertha Elliott and John Beck. There followed a rather hectic morning which soon turned into a council of war—"a council of defense," if you will. Through the confusion we saw what looked like "the writing on the wall," but failed completely to comprehend the cause; and we thought that we must at least ask for a chance to give the vestry an up-to-date account of the work of *The Evangel* office and explain that a magazine, unlike a suitcase, could not be picked up at a moment's notice and carried across the street. Our first concern was how to withstand the pressure in the rector's demand that we move out of "61" and our well-established offices within a month as he prescribed.

He gave me a second, less peremptory call after lunch. The acting senior warden had been in, had been informed, and had left, apparently more wrought up than any of us. We reviewed the various questions raised by his decision less hurriedly than before, and I mentioned the convictions *The Evangel* staff had about the impossibility of moving a magazine in a single month.

Again I returned upstairs, and there significantly enough— across the long table with its piles of letters and manuscripts—sat a young minister named Bruce Larson, a man who had personally found a deeper faith through contact with some of us at Calvary House and who would, in time, himself become an important part of Faith at Work's enlarging staff.

Bruce lovingly offered to drive me home to Princeton where, along with my wife, we reviewed more objectively the unexpected crisis, and then spent the weekend thinking and praying about possible plans of procedure. Everyone involved with the publication expressed a willingness to close down the magazine should this seem advisable. On the other hand, we shared a deep desire to explore the possibilities of saving it and carrying it forward into a new chapter of perhaps larger significance than anything we had known thus far.

Reminding us of Gideon, Bruce suggested that we "put out a fleece"—*two* fleeces in fact. The first would be the whole question of incorporation. At a time when nonprofit organizations had become suspect in New York State because of unscrupulous individuals who were using them for private gain, we would first of all stake the future of our work on the outcome of an attempt to incorporate. Up to that time all of our publishing work had been owned by Calvary Church, New York. The second fleece would concern office space. If God wanted "a magazine of Christian experience" to continue, surely He would lead us to a place where we might work as happily, and perhaps even more freely, than we had in the offices on Gramercy Park. In a short time, such was the urgency and so pertinent these two suggestions that what became known as the Transition Committee immediately adopted these as our first goals.

There followed a rather painful period of uncertainty. We continued and intensified our regular magazine work, but unlike Gideon we got no immediate answers to either of our two pressing questions. Week by week Edward M. Cabaniss, a former warden, called the Transition Committee together in his Manhattan apartment in order to review the situation and report progress if any. One of our committee, J. Daire van Cott, practiced law in the city, and he volunteered to begin to draw up the papers necessary for an application to New York State to incorporate as a nonprofit enterprise. Soon he reported that Ludlow Fowler (another attorney whose son had recently joined the magazine staff), although not a member of Calvary Church, had also offered to help. These men worked quietly but steadily together, and Fowler made at least one trip to Albany to push forward our application. Then, early in the new year, the committee was asked to meet for a private dinner which turned into a hilarious victory celebration, for there before us lay the completed papers of incorporation, signed and sealed by the attorney general of the State. God had answered the question represented by the first fleece with a resounding Yes, and Faith at Work, Inc., had actually come into being. Our name derived from Sam Shoemaker's long insistence that Christianity was "a religion that works."

The search for a new office continued. The rector's own committee had acknowledged the unreasonableness of their earlier demand that we leave Calvary House immediately, and an indefinite extension on the occupancy of our old space had been granted. For awhile it was thought that some other New York church would welcome an ecumenical work such as ours, and we had several pleasant interviews with men like Arthur Kinsolving, Ralph Sockman, and Daniel Poling. In the end, however, it appeared that the amount of space we would need for magazine work alone represented too great an obstacle, so as Easter 1955 came we were still looking.

Meanwhile, the magazine staff sensed a deep concern among the family of subscribers and on the part of many readers to help. We received countless letters of encouragement and had evidence that constant intercessions were being raised throughout the magazine's worldwide fellowship. The number of subscribers sending donations on a monthly basis to meet our operating costs more than doubled.

Late that spring it turned out to be a New Jersey subscriber, Spencer Miller, who came up with an answer to our second crucial need by finding a beautiful, if small, suite of rooms in the building of a friend, just across the street from New York's Public Library. Our new address was to be 8 West 40th Street and our office in a building originally conceived by an enlightened New Yorker who wanted to construct a place suitable to house a United States delegation to the old League of Nations. In mid-summer, with a happy band of volunteers, a borrowed car, and a rented trailer, our Jewish-Christian teacher (whose story appears in Chapter 8), and a new friend, John L. Prescott, a stockbroker, helped the magazine staff to make the move. The total cash outlay came to $16.00!

With a larger staff, which included a sturdy Hollander, Dolf Unger, who had survived a Japanese prison camp experience in Java, and John Haussel, our first paid accountant, the rest of us felt a new commitment to one another as well as a clarification of our purposes and direction. In the business swirl of the new area where we worked we missed the quieter precincts of Gramercy Park, but we had a vigorous new president, Robert W. (Pete) Hudgens, who knew well the uptown pressures of the city. And our unexpected move had drawn in the more active interest and support of people like Mrs. Cleveland E. Dodge and Albert O. Stark, who had both long served as faithful members of the *Evangel* board but now contributed personal suggestions and more of their time.

Our centrally located business office also attracted many casual visitors and subscribers who were just passing through the city. We wanted to meet a wider circle of kindred spirits and we did. Eugenia Price; Dr. Lawrence Murfitt of Kansas; Bermudians whom thus far we had only seen at our conferences; Colonel Robert (Bob) Scott of Michigan; Kirk Cunningham of the "Pittsburgh Experiment"; and Bob Walker, editor of *Christian Life*—these were among the first to drop by.

Daughters of Sam Shoemaker and of Norman Vincent Peale also came on the staff a little later on, plus a young retired colonel of the United States Air Force. After another year or two and, as a kind of cap to our enlarging work team, Bruce Larson agreed to start the whole new department which would expand our conferences.

The space at 8 West 40th Street soon proved far too limited, but fortunately other space became available in the same building and eventually the Christian owner yielded a whole floor, giving us permission to sublet part of the space at a relatively moderate rent. By now our close friend, he simply shook his head saying, "Well, I never expected the sixth floor to go at such a rental but in view of what I see happening I guess I just can't stand in your way."

That sixth floor had a perfectly proportioned conference room which rapidly developed into our most valuable asset. We set Tuesday noon as a time for a men's group, a successor to Calvary's Monday men's meetings; we began a series of teas on Thursdays whose flavor closely resembled the teas at Gramercy Park; and we even started a mixed team with an interlude for an office supper on Monday evenings, 5:30 to 9 o'clock. Two years later a small desk was set up in Bruce's office for none other than our beloved "Sherry" Day. All in all, this period became a rich experience which more than one person described as "too good to be true," and Gramercy Park's loss became 8 West 40th Street's notable gain.

The Participating Churches

On the eve of leaving Gramercy Park I had made a short but rewarding trip to Pittsburgh to see Sam Shoemaker and bring him up to date on the affairs of his old parish, in which he continued to remain vitally interested. He and I both realized that with the considerable new outlays for rent and a larger staff, Faith at Work, Inc., would be more up against it financially than ever *The Evangel* had been, even in our most difficult days. My own plan envisioned enlisting the financial aid, not merely of an increasing number of the generous donors like those who had been keeping us alive through their monthly or yearly contributions, but seeing if there might not be churches which would include *Faith at Work*, as an instrument of evangelism, in their annual budget appeals—as indeed Calvary Church, New York, had finally come to do. In reviewing the scheme in New York staff meetings, Sherry Day, who had been pastor of two Presbyterian churches in the South, was firm in his conviction that such churches existed—both large and small—whose congregations and boards would respond, first because our work was benefiting not a few members in their local congregations, and secondly because of a rapidly growing interest throughout the church in ecumenical work and in evangelism. "Sell it to Sam," said Sherry, adding significantly, "We could call them Participating Churches. They don't join anything different from or outside their own denominations; they will simply be using Faith at Work resources, especially Bruce's weekend conference teams, to help foster what they're already trying to do."

"Participating Churches." We all liked Sherry's designation, and I took the phrase along as the most potent arrow in my quiver in approaching Sam. After all, he had spearheaded and given the work to which we were committed its first major thrust.

Actually Sam had very much wanted us to move the magazine and most of our work out to Pittsburgh and, in fact, he urged this upon several of us, so I knew my approach should be fairly mild. Sure enough his first reaction proved lukewarm. He had a new church and a wealthy one, but all kinds of projects requiring funds were already beginning to blossom under the magic of his leadership. His major focus was now separated entirely from New York. However, he ate up our good news and went so far as to say that he wanted always to be involved in the New York work and especially in any further Calvary conferences, clergy or otherwise.

Then came the (to me) crucial point:

HARRIS: "We've lost a famous address and the protective influence of Calvary Church, New York, but we intend to attempt to go straight ahead and, as you say, function not as an agency parallel to the church but as a vital, active force for evangelism and outreach right within the Body of Christ. We're not in Pittsburgh as a staff but we feel as much a part of your ministry as ever. We want to help, but of course, we'll *need* help, especially with what you've sometimes dubbed 'the sinews of war.'"

SHOEMAKER: "You've always been able to stand financially pretty much on your own. In Pittsburgh we will certainly advertise the magazine and solicit subscriptions. What else can we do?"

HARRIS: "Sherry Day has suggested a new category for churches like yours where there's such keenness about evangelism. He, like the rest of us, wants to link up the strong and the weak, call a few of the congregations closest to us Participating Churches and ask them to take up some of the slack in the greatly increased budget."

SHOEMAKER: "I like Sherry's word 'participating.' I'm sure the vestry here will approve of our working closely with you in such a capacity. How much of a financial contribution would you want us to make?"

HARRIS (gulping): "A thousand dollars."

SHOEMAKER: "That's quite a sum. I do have access to some limited special funds, but I'll have to think this one over."

The next day, bright and early over the breakfast table, Sam leaned forward and, with a characteristic twinkle, volunteered, "About the money, you can have it."

And so came into existence the first of the new Participating Churches of Faith at Work, Inc. Within six months we had nine others—two of them in New York, St. James Episcopal and Rutgers Presbyterian—and shortly Marble Collegiate Church as well. None were able to give as generously as Calvary Church, Pittsburgh, nor should they have, because in a way Faith at Work was still to some extent a Shoemaker baby.

The other new assistance which seemed to come "straight from on high" was what I called wholesale promotion. This resulted from the vision of a few farsighted Christian businessmen who believed that, if larger groups of people, missionaries as well as laymen, could be given a chance to see copies of the *Faith at Work* magazine, a good many in such fields would want to subscribe. The way it worked is illustrated by the initiative of a Brooklyn manufacturer who had a drop-forging plant in Astoria. Merrill Gardner quietly wrote to the headquarters of the mission boards of three large churches—the North American Baptist Conference was one—and suggested that if he were furnished with a list of their overseas workers, he would have sample copies of "The Magazine of Christian Experience" sent, with a covering letter to each missionary. He further offered to pay for gift subscriptions for those who responded by writing that they would like to receive the magazine regularly. Affirmative letters full of interest and gratitude flowed in and the *Faith at Work* magazine began to penetrate areas where we had never gone before. A country like Zambia, for instance, would turn up Christian workers who needed more illustrations of the "how" of Christian faith, which was our specialty, and in certain instances new subscribers would ask permission to excerpt and use our stories, often in mimeographed form, in their own local, native-language publications. The outreach from New York thereby often increased in a twofold way.

In a somewhat similar manner a few great, nationally known editors like E. J. Meeman of the *Press Scimitar* in Memphis, Tennessee; and David Lawrence of the *U.S. News and World Report*, in Washington, D.C., remitted substantial sums "that this witness may continue and its scope widened." Ed Meeman had a special keenness to cover the costs of non-Americans in places like the leper colonies of the Philippines—people who simply could never pay for *Faith at Work* themselves.

16 /
Where a Man Works

*W*hen it became clear that more time was needed to help men with the pressure and competitiveness of their business lives than was available at our Monday groups, Sam Shoemaker suggested a series of Saturday morning seminars. These meetings were well publicized under the title "School of Life for Business and Professional Men."

It attracted new faces and many individuals who had no official connection with Calvary Church. On one particular Saturday as I was reviewing a number of Jesus' Parables and their relation to the commercial and political life of the twentieth century, my attention was caught by a handsome, silver-haired latecomer seated in the back row. He seemed to follow what was said with unusual attentiveness. When the meeting broke up, I introduced myself and met Edward M. Cabaniss for the first time. When I discovered that he lived but a few blocks from Gramercy Park, I described our Monday businessmen's gatherings and urged him to come to one of them.

The very next Monday, in came Ed Cabaniss, a little on the late side but not at all shy about drawing a chair into the circle. At the first pause he was asked to introduce himself and it turned out that he was an officer of the Dixon Crucible Company of Jersey City, one of whose products was the familiar yellow Ticonderoga lead pencil. In referring to the Saturday meeting, he spoke quite frankly about his need for a stronger personal faith and his desire to have the company run along Christian lines. He admitted that he had been on the vestries of several Episcopal churches, "But you know," he went on, "I'm not satisfied with putting on a cutaway and passing the plate on Sundays." As a ripple of laughter touched the group, he went on to say that he thought business was one of God's vineyards. After all, he pointed out, the office is the place where a man spends most of his waking hours, and if he has any faith it should be a mighty good place to put it to work. He would like to know how to go about it. Across the circle another businessman quietly suggested that the place for anyone to begin was with himself.

Then at the same meeting, on a Monday about a month later, our pencil company executive was asked if he would care to give a progress report. And sure enough Mr. Cabaniss was more than ready to do just that: "I took the advice someone gave and decided that I *would* start with myself. I've always believed in prayer but, after listening to two or three of you describe your own daily devotions, I saw I simply wasn't taking enough time for my own prayer life. For instance, I saw I'd have to get up earlier in the morning or nothing of consequence would happen. I began to set the alarm for six o'clock."

On another Monday he spoke more directly about his office: "A short prayer on arrival, asking God's help with what waits right there on my desk for me to tackle, has proved a tremendous blessing. It's surprising the many ways the power of evil can invade my mind, causing me to become resentful, or irritated, or even a prey to fear. I so easily act without due consideration for those about me. But by trying to live close to Jesus Christ I can almost count on His stepping in and helping me, at any moment and no matter what the problem. I also find it a great help to pray before entering a board meeting or a business conference, naming some of those who will take part and especially the person or persons whose views I fear may conflict with my own."

One Monday, a few weeks later, Ed Cabaniss told the following story of an out-of-town trip with his executive vice president:

"Frank Atchinson and I were up in the Adirondacks inspecting an old graphite mine and sharing a hotel room for the night. When it came time to turn the lights out, I realized with surprise how terribly timid I still was about my new-found faith. 'Frank,' I said hesitatingly, 'I've been experimenting with more personal prayer, both night and morning to be exact.' But I got no further, for with a laugh my associate at once spoke up. 'Ed, I think that's great! Just let me join you.' There we were, almost before I realized what was happening, asking the help of Almighty God for ourselves, for our loved ones, and for the company. And in the morning the greatest idea came to us as we again thought about the company: *Why not have a group, something like this Monday one, but meeting monthly, and ask the head of each department in the company to join us?* I believe they will. And before long I'll hope to let you fellows know how things go."

The full story came out piecemeal. These two men started something which not merely brought a new quality of life into the company but at a later crisis saved their company from being destroyed; and much that they poineered month by month suggested business procedures which influenced more than a few other industrial concerns.

At the beginning they simply invited seven other men, each a department head, to a monthly dinner "to think together and pray about the company." A nearby hotel rather than the plant restaurant was purposely chosen as their rendezvous. One associate drew back at first on the grounds that he was "not a praying man," but being given a further invitation he reconsidered, and then at the third gathering asked the chairman if he might have the privilege of giving the "invocation!" The important point was that, right from the start, there was a remarkable sense of freedom. The youngest man in the group, the manager of personnel, announced that he wanted to bring up a company practice which had always bothered him but which, without the new group, he had felt too shy to mention. He asked one question: "Why must Dixon employees be designated by numbers instead of by their real names?" Why indeed? Although everyone at the table laughed, they caught a fresh view of their employees as people. Not long afterwards the entire bookkeeping system of the venerable concern was revolutionized, with names of employees replacing numbers.

It happened to be this same personnel director who, a little later, quietly challenged the company's system of discharging individuals for misconduct. Jersey City has never been noted for its elevated morals, but Jack Hamilton became the first Dixon official to make a detailed study of the city's social service agencies, discovering, for instance, how active Alcoholics Anonymous had become in several areas. With the backing of the monthly group, he next persuaded the company's employee superintendent to send duplicate discharge slips to his office, and before a person who had been blacklisted for something like drinking was actually fired, such an individual was offered a personal interview if he chose to have one. As a result, more than one man soon found help which led to their reinstatement.

Two other members of the group, the chief of sales and the head of production, then had important matters of long-standing disagreement which were solved by frank, private discussions. Through a better understanding of their constantly changing markets and the competitive conditions in the industry, those responsible for production went so far as to agree to basic changes in a number of the company's chief products. Finally there came an evening when the production and sales chiefs could laugh and agree that the production lines were coming up with a list of fully marketable items.

Not wishing to interject too personal an influence on the group, Mr. Cabaniss, now president of the company, decided to let things ride. Two months passed with no meetings. Then he was asked directly by one of the group if something was the matter. "No," he replied, "but I simply don't want to press these meetings unless the rest of you want them." His colleague answered with mingled amusement and alarm: "Want them! Now, listen, you simply can't stop the meetings now!" So month by month they continued, and gradually the spirit of the group spread among the rank and file and the company became "the family."

One special crisis—coming unexpectedly as crises often do—left no question of this. The general counsel, or legal representative, of the company was approached by the agent of a wealthy clique of Manhattan financiers with an offer to buy eighty-five percent of the Joseph E. Dixon Crucible Company stock at a price somewhat higher than the then market value but considerably less than its *true* value. When this offer was refused, the same clique purchased the few hundred shares of stock they could lay their hands on. Then they successfully obtained a court order to secure the full list of company stockholders with a view to soliciting all of them and acquiring at least fifty-one percent of the company's securities.

When notified of this, the monthly group of nine Dixon officers called a special meeting for special prayer. They then informed the entire body of employees of what was afoot and of the danger of the company changing hands, with a chance of possible liquidation. At the same time they reminded the rank and file of the well-established stock-sharing plan through which anybody in the company could buy his own stock. Within a week a group of employees who already owned stock formed their own committee and quickly planned to back up the current management. Then they, too, applied for a full list of stockholders' names and addresses. Not only this; the employee committee raised a sum of money from among their fellows in the plant and promptly got out a letter. They explained the probability that an offer would soon be made by an outside group to buy up workers' stock but that they, as Dixon employees, would match any price the New York group set, as far as their resources would go. In the end the outside faction offered seventy dollars a share and cannily reserved the right to return the stock if they failed to secure a majority interest. Actually they secured only ten per cent of the stock outstanding, while the number of employees holding Dixon stock tripled within a month—and, of course, the company remained under its old management.

The annual meeting that year, which occurred soon thereafter, might have been an explosive one in the wake of so much tension and opposing plans, but in Ed Cabaniss's words, "It turned out to be almost a love feast." Before breakfast on the very day of the meeting, Mr. Cabaniss received a 'phone call from the wife of one of the men in the plant, asking the exact time of the meeting. The woman explained that she and her close friends intended to be in the chapel in a New York hotel at that time in order to pray for the company when the meeting was in progress.

On becoming chairman of the board of the company Mr. Cabaniss summed up his personal philosophy of business in these words: "It seems to me to be perfectly logical that people in industry should pray to Almighty God for guidance for and in their work. Millions of God's children earn their livelihood in that branch of society. We pray for better education and abundant agriculture. I believe we should also pray for the welfare of industry. I now have the conviction that our problems, whether they be personal, family, political, or social, will only be met as God comes into our lives, individually and collectively. I for one intend to carry on as best I can as a soldier of Christ in industry."

The Judge's Story*

There is much in the Bible about judges, but I do not recall any occasion on which a judge has been called upon to discuss the impact of religion upon the performance of the judicial function. Perhaps this is because this is an intimate matter—thoughts about which one is likely to keep to one's self.

I suppose I am a more or less typical American. From boyhood I have had an implicit and unquestioning faith, which I got when I attended the classes in the Episcopal Church at Ossining, New York, in preparation for my confirmation. Like most other people I know, I wanted to be a better Christian but, as I look back over the years, I find that I did comparatively little to put this wishful thinking into effect.

As a law student and as a lawyer, I fought hard for what I thought was right, and I had a deep and almost passionate interest in the rules of law and the history of their development. They were the tools of my trade and I worked hard with them.

It was not long after I became a judge that I began to feel a new sense of responsibility. It is something very difficult to explain. It was not simply that I wanted to be right and that I took my duties seriously. There came a feeling that everything I did, even the decision of nice questions of interpretation of mere rules of procedure, was in some way becoming a part of a huge fabric which on the whole was part and parcel of the moral law governing mankind and which must of necessity be of divine origin.

As I passed upon the credibility of witnesses and as I wrote my opinions and formulated my judgments, I gradually came to realize that I was weaving my small part of this huge fabric; and I knew that I would not perform my task aright unless I was constantly mindful of the fact that all these matters, large and small, would be mere futility unless I tried to make each one fit into its proper place in the moral law which governed all.

Right here is the part that is difficult to explain. I was still reasoning as a lawyer. The fundamental principles of law were the same. I was still manipulating the techniques of my profession as

---

* This article is part of an address given by Harold R. Medina, former judge of the District Court of the United States for the Southern District of New York, before the Church Club of New York and later reprinted by permission in both *The Living Church* and *Evangel* magazines.

before. But there was some subtle force, the impact of which was new to me, which was spiritual in quality. It was as though someone were always watching me and telling me to make very sure that my rulings and my decisions were fundamentally right and just.

You know we judges are the servants of the people, as are all government officials in our particular type of democracy. But I think it will not be difficult for you to see from the things I have been telling you about that it didn't take me very long to perceive that we judges are servants of Someone Else, too.

Fortunately for me, I was taught to pray from so early a time that I cannot remember going to bed at night without saying my prayers. And only once in all these years have I failed to do so. I remember that occasion very vividly. It was my first night in boarding school, when I was about fourteen years old. And in all the excitement of my room at school and my new roommate, and in the general bewilderment, I forgot to say my prayers.

Now I need not tell you that the toughest part of the judge's work is sentencing the people who are convicted or who plead guilty to the various offenses. I had always wondered what I should do if at the time of sentence some prisoner was impudent to me. It seems so clear that in the stress of such an occasion the judge should not mete out a greater punishment from some feeling of personal pique.

One day this happened to me. You may not know it, but the fact is that, of the millions of government checks that go out through the mail from day to day, many are placed in mail boxes on the ground floor of "walk-up" apartment houses and furnish a constant temptation to people in distress, or to those of naturally predatory instincts. Most of the time they get caught and, as it is a federal offense, they come before the judges of my court.

On this particular occasion a woman who was soon to become a mother came before me, and I struggled away with the probation report and with questions to see what I should do. She suddenly burst out and gave me a tongue lashing that was a work of art. After reflecting for a moment or two, I made up my mind that it would not be right to sentence her that day, and so, over her resounding protests, I put the matter off for a week.

The following Sunday I was sitting in my pew at St. James' Church, New York, when the rector, at a certain point in the service, said that he would pause for a moment or two so that every member of the congregation could make a silent prayer in connection with whatever matter was troubling him. I prayed for that woman just as hard and as fervently as I knew how.

A day or two later, she was back there in court standing before me. I told her all about what I had been going through; I told her that I had prayed for her in church. And the outcome was that I gave her a suspended sentence. I do not think there is very much chance that she will be in my court or any other court again.

I do not see why a judge should be ashamed to say that he prays for divine guidance and for strength to do his duty. Indeed, there came a time not so long after the incident I have just described, when I did the most sincere and the most fervent praying that I ever did in my life.

I suddenly found myself in the midst of the trial of the American Communists. It took me a long time to realize what they were trying to do to me. But as I got weaker and weaker, and found the burden difficult to bear, I sought strength from the one source that never fails.

Let me be specific. There came a time when, doubtless due to previous planning, one of the defendants on the stand refused to answer a question, pleading a supposed constitutional privilege which obviously had no application. I gave him time to consult with his counsel. I held the matter in abeyance overnight to make sure that I was making no misapplication of the law, and then, the next day, I sentenced him to prison for thirty days, unless he should purge himself of contempt by answering the question.

Pandemonium broke loose. The other ten defendants and their lawyers, and many of the spectators, rose to their feet; there was a great shouting and hullabaloo, and several of the defendants started toward the bench.

In all that excitement, I felt just as calm as I do now. I did not raise my voice, and I singled out several of those men, identified the language they were using, got it on the record, and sentenced each of them to imprisonment for the balance of the trial.

My unguided will alone, and such self-control as I possess, were unequal to this test. If ever a man felt the presence of Someone beside him, strengthening his will and giving him aid and comfort, it was I on that day.

And so it was later, when I finally left the courtroom one day and went to lie down, thinking that perhaps I should never go back. But, after ten or fifteen minutes, I was refreshed and I did go back; and I gained in strength from that moment to the end.

After all is said and done, it is not we who pull the strings; we are not the masters but the servants of our Master's will; and it is well that we should know it to be so.

The Stockbroker

John Ryder was in advertising. He had expanded his New York firm by offering a syndicated service to provide small-town builders and construction people with advertising copy for their local newspapers. It was a family business and John was president.

His personal needs had brought him into contact with a men's group at Calvary Church and with Alcoholics Anonymous groups there and in the suburb where he lived. He was a great admirer of Sam Shoemaker and at the latter's encouragement had participated, one summer, in an Oxford Group house party in England. On his return he started a daily Bible-study group in his Madison Avenue office to which he invited his staff and a few other businessmen. Attendance was purely voluntary and those who met came early so as not to interfere with the company's office routine.

One spring morning a handsome, middle-aged stockbroker showed up at the group rather unexpectedly. He and John Ryder, as commuters, sometimes sat together coming into the city on an early train, and the visitor had heard about the group in that way. He was another John, named Prescott, and on this particular morning he was wearing a rather loud checked suit as if dressed for the races.

The discussion got rather lively that day, in a give-and-take fashion, and John Prescott seemed to like what he heard. When the group broke up, John Ryder grabbed his arm. "Say," he remarked, "you really got into it this morning."

"Yeah," said John of the checked suit. "It was good. I guess I needed it."

After a minute, Prescott continued, hesitatingly, "How did you get going yourself in this kind of a life? How does a fellow make one of these 'surrenders' you talk about? Sounds to me a bit like throwing in the towel. I don't like the word."

"No, no." Ryder spoke with a slight stutter. " 'Surrender' is n-n-nothing like that at all. It's the way I found out how to get my own mind off liquor—and plenty of other things, too, which were messing me up."

"H-m-m." Then, after a pause, Prescott said thoughtfully, "As a matter of fact, as the result of something I heard at church, I decided just the other day to commit my own life to God, but I haven't the foggiest idea how to do it."

John Ryder smiled warmly. They were now alone and he suggested they sit down again. "That would make a tremendous difference," he began. There followed a pause. "Look," he went on, "almost around the corner on Gramercy Park, there's a friend of mine named Sam Shoemaker. Go over and see him, will you? He'll t-t-tell you the *how* of things like this. How to 'let go and let God,' as he puts it. He's a great fellow. You'll like him."

What may have been a half-hour later, John Prescott arrived at 61 Gramercy Park. He asked for the rector. The girl at the switchboard said he had gone out but suggested the inquirer go up to Room 403 and see Irving Harris.

My editorial endeavors were suddenly interrupted by a thunderous bang on the door. Somewhat irritated at this unannounced interruption I swung my swivel chair around and impatiently called, "Yes? Come in." There stood Prescott, checked suit and all.

The handsome visitor stepped into the room and hesitantly explained that John Ryder had sent him over to see the rector. By this time I had recovered myself. "I'm glad you dropped in," I said. "Sam Shoemaker is out of the building, but perhaps there's something I can do for you." John Prescott had taken a chair. He paused a moment and then leaning forward and riveting me with his eyes said, 'I want to make a complete surrender of my life to Jesus Christ."

The editor of a magazine on evangelism may well talk with more than a few people who are moving toward conversion, but I had never heard a successful businessman put his desire for personal, spiritual revolution so bluntly.

"That's a rather drastic step," I said. "Can you tell me a little about yourself? What work do you do? What family have you? What you suggest involves a good many things. Committing one's life to God is more than a personal resolution to live a better life."

"I know that and I've tried many times to straighten my problems out by myself. It doesn't work, even with the help of the doctors. My wife and I are again on the verge of a divorce. She is an alcoholic but very allergic to A.A. I and my daughters at times have been wonderfully blest by God, but we have had our problems, too. And not long ago my business partner and I had a terrible bust up. All in all, my life has suddenly become a total mess. You could say I'm coming to God for purely selfish reasons, for that's the truth. I not only want His help, I need it—desperately."

After this we talked for half an hour or so, and when the associate who shared my office came in I asked him to join us. We were both aware that our visitor's problems were by no means unrelated to our own lives. Besides, the fact that a comparative stranger could so honestly and openly entrust us with such personal concerns stirred in us a sense of humility.

Then the stockbroker rather abruptly asked, "Well, where do we go from here?"

It was easy for me to take the cue. I pointed to a sofa at the side of the room. "Would you by any chance like to pray with the two of us?" I said. He nodded, and in a moment he simply poured his heart out to God in the first spoken prayer of his life. Then the other two of us prayed briefly for him—and ourselves.

And so it happened. A sense of peace and promise had settled in that room. As we stood up, the stockbroker's face unmistakably told of the active power of the living God and of his own awareness that the new chance he wanted had been granted to him. I reached out my hand. John Prescott grabbed it in a way that made words unnecessary. "Don't come downstairs," he said. "I may stop in the church on my way back to the office."

Some months passed during which the stockbroker made many significant contributions to the Monday men's group, including this story of his own new commitment to God. Matters eased for him at home and on Wall Street. There were the usual luncheons and personal 'phone calls, but, spiritually speaking, John Prescott had a Chapter Two which focused on "George," his estranged partner. From the day he had felt the new lease on his own life, the ancient animosity with George rankled the more and cried out for some kind of treatment. Everything negative that had been done or said on either side seemed important now only in that it had spoiled a relationship which in the main had been a good one. John realized that a healing step could be taken and that he was the one to make the first move. What cried out in his heart were not the details, the pros and cons, but rather the new factor that he himself felt contrite and sorry.

Then the day came when he went to George's office, half hoping to see him and half hoping he'd be out. John says that he paced to and fro in the corridor before George's door for some little while, hesitating, before he finally took the plunge, turned the knob on the door, and entered.

George looked up from his desk, startled. He was sitting directly opposite the door and great was his surprise to see his old partner there again before him. He felt considerably taken aback at the abruptness of his appearance—and well he might have. But suddenly it struck him that John's attitude had something special in it. As he rose to greet him, John simply thrust out a big hand and in a voice charged with emotion spoke the few words he felt most deeply: "I'm so sorry, George, so sorry. Will you forgive me?"

Forgive him? Now it was George's turn to be moved. "John," he replied with the sincerity of a man revealing his deepest feelings, "thank you, thank you, dear fellow. I've so often hoped against hope that something like this would happen, and now you've said the very thing I want to say myself."

As they stood there facing each other across George's desk, all the past conflict evaporated and was forgotten, and something warm and new caught and held them. They never did discuss the old problems. It seemed unnecessary. A friendship was reborn, and the magic words "I'm sorry" completely bridged the gulf of time and space and healed the wound forever. From that day forward a close, creative relationship existed between them, unbreakable and mutually enriching. Among other results, John Prescott shortly became a director of Faith at Work, Inc.

17/
An Enlarging Staff
with a Growing Edge

As the Pocono conferences gained in popularity and the magazine's outreach increased, an ever heavier load fell on the small New York staff. We enjoyed the new offices but I began to wonder how we could carry the work forward without considerably enlarging our new nonprofit organization, and funds seemed to be lacking for this. The board of directors took a serious view of this question and individual members volunteered special financial assistance. We shortly found both a young assistant editor and a full-time accountant. Even so, several of us still seemed far too busy, and as a staff we lacked an adequate plan to provide for the increasing number of invitations from "participating" and other churches.

At the invitation of some close friends who formed a businessmen's group in Bermuda I went down there for a week to think things over. The fellowship with the Bermudians gave me a lift, and we had one small crucial team meeting at a director's guest house, "Rosedon," on the eve of my return.

"The easiest plan," I explained, "would be to terminate the magazine, despite our successful incorporation. The new office has increased our budget and added to our general work load, and this makes impossible an adequate plan to multiply the programing of conference weekends." The fact was that the pressure of additional editing had robbed my own work of its freshness and I would have welcomed an "out." But any idea of discontinuing *Faith at Work* magazine met immediate, vocal opposition. As one man put it, "If you and Bertha Elliott should quit at this point, you would let us all down and cancel out the great advances God has given through the new office, the help of the Participating Churches, and the constant growth of the magazine family."

"No, you've no right to stop now," said another. "Instead, look for a man to take over the conference work, including the Poconos, and free you and the magazine staff for exclusive attention to your regular publishing duties."

"That sounds right," volunteered a third. "Do you happen to know someone who could come to us as a conference director and develop that special side of the work?"

"Yes," I had to admit, "there is such a man who, by his past performance at Gramercy Park and at the Poconos, has shown his capacity to do just this. His name is Bruce Larson and he is a young Presbyterian minister who might or might not be interested in taking on such an assignment."

We had some prayer. The strong, general consensus of the group was that I should at once contact Bruce Larson and sound him out on the possibility of his becoming our conference director.

I flew back to New York the next day determined to continue as magazine editor and at the same time put up to Bruce the crying need and great opportunity of this new work. That year he was serving as pastor of a church in the small town of Pana in south central Illinois. I had no idea of his plans, but I knew that he had a deep interest in our Faith at Work witness meetings and "house parties." His own life and ministry had been vitally affected by the work at Calvary House and he had taken a leading part in the first Pocono conference. But I felt I needed to see him face to face if I were to give him an adequate picture of both the need and the opportunity now opening up for Faith at Work "conference work."

The map showed that Decatur, Illinois, was the largest city near Pana and in an hour or two I had reserved a hotel room there, plus a drive-yourself car, and I had bought a round-trip plane ticket for my first venture into that section of the Midwest. And an adventure it did turn out to be! An early December snowstorm greeted me in Decatur, my bag was lost at the O'Hare Field in Chicago, and when I phoned the Larsons in the morning, a Saturday, I was told that they were out of town! No one but my wife knew where I was and I foresaw that my report to her might well turn out to be the story of a wild goose chase. However, I spent the day visiting another Faith at Work family in the area, trusting that the Larsons would return before the weekend was out. And of course they did. We spent most of Sunday together, and my account of coming to them as fast as possible, straight from the meeting in Bermuda, spoke as eloquently, I believe, as any of the details I described about Faith at Work's new outreach.

But how were we to open up a new department if the whole venture was financially still so "touch and go." I was able to assure them that three of our directors were ready to underwrite a small salary for them for at least two years, and that before long, so keen was the demand for conference help, I believed a whole raft of new friends would appear and support such a special project. I told them of the enthusiastic backing of the Bermudians and underlined the old principle, well-tested by this time, that "where God guides He provides." Acutally it took Bruce and Hazel Larson several months to get their own "green light" to undertake this work, but by the end of the summer all was clear and they had found a home to use as a pied-a-terre for Bruce in Westfield, New Jersey.

Nothing in Faith at Work ever exhibited more visible signs of the "breeze of the spirit" than Bruce's new job. His correspondence increased alarmingly and churches of almost every denomination wrote us at 8 West 40th Street asking for conferences. To deal with the demands, and as the result of prayerful insights, Bruce established several basic guidelines. One was to require proof of the existence of a local team in the area where a conference was to be held; or, to put it another way, no conferences were to be scheduled just because a clergyman, or some small committee, felt a conference would pep up a spiritually dead situation. So it happened that many a conference only took place several months or even a year after it was first asked for, a group of some kind being formed meantime to get into action.

Secondly, Bruce consistently refused to act in the capacity of a "big speaker." The leadership of all conferences centered in a team, of which Bruce was often but not necessarily a member. Lay people who had had conference experience either at Gramercy Park or at the Poconos were enlisted as a corps both to provide the chief speakers at the various weekends and to take responsibility for the workshops, which soon became so important in presenting Christian truth at the conferences. Experienced teammates were also to act as leaders of the "talk-it-over-groups" which formed the smaller units of the conferences and in which everyone who attended a conference had the chance to speak, to ask questions, and to pray.

Within the first year conferences took place in New England and down South in centers like Montgomery, Alabama. The next year, special, larger events developed, such as a conference sponsored by two Presbyterian churches in Pittsburgh which required a team of sixty-five or seventy. In other parts of the country strong churches like The First Baptist Church in Sioux Falls, South Dakota, under the leadership of Roger Fredrikson, held immense meetings and soon generated enough changed lives to be able to answer requests themselves for the leadership of conferences in various other sections. Not long after, with much of the expense borne by Californians, a team at Asilomar on the Monterey Peninsula held a weekend rivaling in numbers and quality the original Pocono conferences in Pennsylvania.

Larger and larger local teams appeared in these various sections generating their own top leadership, and thus it came about that some twenty or more field representatives were chosen to take special responsibility for Faith at Work activities in all the separate areas, and to synchronize these with a national schedule. Then, of necessity, these field representatives began to gather at least once a year with Bruce and others in New York in order to evaluate results, clarify emphases, and consolidate the national work as a whole.

*   *   *

Genie Price, the author, gives a picture of our life in the new office at 8 West 40th Street, in an article she wrote for the May 1960 issue of *Christian Life* magazine:

The other day I sat in an editorial office on 40th Street in New York City. Things were quiet and unhurried. There was good, easy conversation and occasional real laughter. Most important, God was there and no one seemed surprised. He is always expected.

The editor and the Rev. Bruce Larson, Faith at Work's new Field Representative, had just come in from a weekly luncheon at The

Princton Club and were still glowing from the impact of the meeting. Both had been with Christ and it showed. They started to talk about their unique magazine and its outreach.

"It's much more than a magazine," the editor spoke my own thoughts. "It is a living organism. The printed pages are merely our means of keeping 'the family' informed of what Christ is doing. Our mail, which is enormous in proportion to our circulation, shows unmistakably that we are reaching men and women and young people from all walks of life. We like to think that the Faith at Work 'family' is a small sampling of what Kingdom living really is."

I opened an issue of the magazine at random and came upon an account of a lady writing her own story. She said in part:

"I was beginning to think this business of religion would be a pretty good thing—for some people I knew! And so I tried to straighten out my husband and my neighbors. Of course, I didn't help anybody, and all the time kept getting more snarled up inside. I was a mess! One day I had to admit I was defeated and desperate. I had sought the advice of friends, taken medicines, gone to doctors and psychologists—everything, in fact, except 'seeking first the Kingdom.'

"At last I broke down and agreed to attend group meetings, and there I found people who had already discovered God, who were trying to live with Him daily, and who furthermore cared about my needs. I came with *my* burdens but found that, as I began to take *theirs*, mine became lighter.

"Gradually I yielded parts of my life to Christ, some of them over and over again, until I finally surrendered myself—the whole works. The atmosphere in our home changed. I used to be afraid to be alone at night. That fear is gone. I used to *eat* pills. Now I don't. The bickering at home has disappeared. I have a whole new outlook and a new life."

Each issue of *Faith at Work* carries such candid portraits of human life made whole by personal encounters with Jesus Christ. Young beatniks, alcoholics, irritable housewives, successful but high-strung business executives, teachers, nurses, doctors, professional people—some famous, all people for whom Christ died.

The editor went on talking in the quiet comfortable little offices in New York. "We're rather proud," he said, "of the fact that from reading our magazine no one can spot a predominant group or denomination. With all our hearts we long for the magazine to hold up Jesus Christ and Him crucified and risen. That's all there is, really, isn't there?

He went on. "We are vitally interested in healing, in prayer, in the deeper life. But personal and group evangelism—that is, doing all we can do to lift up Christ to those who don't know Him—is our main motivation. We simply use the device Jesus used. We tell stories which people can understand."

Thus the magazine is not the main interest of the Faith at Work group. It is a living organism, part of the group's outreach to the English-speaking world—one of the channels God is using to touch the hearts of those to whom English is sometimes an unwieldy, very foreign language.

An insurance executive in Nova Scotia is typical. He had recently written the editor: "This, I hope, is not going to be a sermon, but I want you to know that your magazine has helped me to come back again to Christ. I have been so busy lately, rushing here and there, getting very little accomplished. Forgetting my prayer time and never listening for guidance. Then last night I felt I needed something more than just the evening paper or the stock quotations, so I picked up your magazine and read 'He Never Leaves Me,' by Dick Taliaferro. I just had to get down on my knees and thank God for putting up with the likes of me. This morning I had to drop you a line to ask you to renew my subscription. . . . Yesterday things looked awfully gray. However, this morning's sunrise was the most beautiful I have ever seen. My most sincere thanks. Court Baker."

Such letters pour in daily—from people in Bible institutes; Christian and secular universities; from ministers, professional and business people; teen-agers and their parents. Each one is acknowledged and if help is asked, help is given. There are those on the Faith at Work staff whose responsibility it is to see that every request is followed up. Much time is spent in prayer each day at the office—prayer for the conversion of those who need Christ, prayer for healing, both emotional and physical, prayer for guidance and wisdom.

But everything is not done by mail by any means. In New York City, usually at Rutgers Presbyterian Church, regular Faith at Work meetings are held. I have spoken at one of these meetings, and there were more people from more walks of life and more varied Christian backgrounds and churches than I have ever encountered. Instead of the hypo variety of pumped-up fervor, there was the deep, natural sense of the Spirit's Presence, which I have come to expect when I am with a Faith at Work group anywhere. We sang a long time, but no one needed to jack us up. We felt like singing!

As the circulation of the magazine grows, the personal contacts increase. Faith at Work meetings are no longer limited to New York City. This is because God found an obedient and surprising young man named Bruce Larson, who was willing to give up the comfortable pastorate of a growing church and become a twentieth-century traveling apostle. He goes with a team of, as he says, "just people like me."

Although he is on a modest salary, his team usually pays its own expenses. Two may go with him or eighteen, as happened recently in New England. They accept an invitation from the minister of a church, stay in the homes of the members, and guide the simple audience-participation, witnessing, sharing, and discussion meetings in the church. Or even more important, off-beat sessions held in someone's office or living room.

"The Spirit seems delighted to get us together anywhere at any time. He never fails to meet us," says Larson. Lives are being changed wherever these "team visits" take place. Ministers themselves write of their own changed lives. Nominal church members are being converted to Christ. Prayer groups are springing up in offices and homes and factories.

At the end of May each year there is a Faith at Work conference in the Pocono Mountains. It, too, began small. Last year hundreds of people came, some from foreign countries.

*　　*　　*

After a further year or two the staff took over the entire sixth floor at 8 West 40th Street. At this point no Manhattanite frequented the—to us—gorgeous new offices more regularly than Bob Arnold. His small studio apartment was now but a few blocks away and as a portrait painter and man-about-town his daily schedule showed marked flexibility. He had already started setting aside a prized, early hour for personal devotions—more conscientiously, perhaps than any of us. Clearly he was enjoying this experiment of being "under new management"—that was his secret. As part of his new schedule, he rarely missed one of Bryant Kirkland's Sunday services at the Fifth Avenue Presbyterian Church where he quickly formed a score of new friendships.

The girls on our switchboard were never surprised to see Bob pop in, morning, noon, or night. But it was a little before noon on Tuesday that we came to expect him "without fail." That was the day of the men's meeting, a direct offspring of the old Monday meeting at Calvary House. Once Bob had discovered the fellowship of the staff and the New York business neighbors who drifted in for this Tuesday meeting, he rarely missed it or the short, preparatory half-hour which preceded the main gathering. He was spiritual dynamite on the New York team, dropping a suggestion or a humorous remark one week and perhaps telling an arresting story the next. He quickly became one of those extras whom Sam Shoemaker had always had on the staff at Gramercy Park, and he rated a high priority with us because, above all else, he was and still is that somewhat rare bird, a sure-enough evangelist.

* * *

Robert Waite Arnold, a native of Delaware, had interrupted his career as a portrait painter by service in the United States Army in World War II. He had emerged as a Major. But let Wally Howard, who had become editor of *Faith at Work* magazine about a year before Bob made his appearance, give the full story of his conversion as he wrote is up in a notable, blow-by-blow account, entitled "My Friend Bob," in our March 1964 issue:

In 1961 Bob Arnold put his studio apartment on 58th Street up for lease. He had moved back to New York when his marriage broke up. The divorce had triggered a deep distrust in himself. Three sessions a week for a year with a psychiatrist helped to reassure him, but these did not displace the loneliness or end his search to know what was wrong.

He was not painting. The inner well of inspiration had gone dry. Occasionally he would pause in a church to pray, but more often he relied on tranquilizers and martinis to keep him going. Then bill collectors began to pressure him and he put his apartment up for rent.

Joan Gibbons, a delightful fashion model from England, along with many others, came to see the apartment and Bob showed her around. "You'll like it," he assured her. "It's very quiet. The only noise is on Sundays." He pointed to the back wall. "Through there is the organ of a church. You can hear it on Sunday mornings."

"Oh, that's my church," Joan smiled. "Calvary Baptist. Why don't you visit us sometime?"

Attend a church service? Bob couldn't have cared less. At fourteen, in Delaware, he had joined a church. It was the thing to do. Over the years he had listened to an occasional radio preacher. And he had visited churches to admire their art. He had even painted his conception of Christ for a Presbyterian church on Long Island. But he had long ago stopped attending services. One would scarcely expect to find God in a church service!

Joan persisted, and finally Bob went. The people were "nice," and there was coffee afterward.

Two years later, Joan called to tell of something special coming to her church. People from all over the world would be telling their own personal stories. The theme, "Under New Management," intrigued him. He went and sat with Joan through the opening meeting and was moved even more by some of the stories.

Then people were then assigned to small talk-it-over groups, according to the number on their name tags. When Bob sensed that he was to go in one direction and Joan in another, he panicked: "Don't leave me with these people," he whispered. So she steered him to her own group, which Sherry Day was leading.

When they introduced themselves around the circle, Bob said, quite honestly, "I'm searching." Sherry picked it up at once and when the meeting broke up his hand was on Bob's arm. "So you're searching. That's wonderful. Let's have a chat." The chat lasted two hours and Sherry's words made sense. The God who made the universe surely could manage Bob's life. But surrender to Him? Surrender his freedom?

The next night in his studio, Bob decided to try. He got on his knees and prayed, but nothing seemed to happen. So on Sunday he went back to the conference in search of Sherry. The meetings were just breaking up and Sherry was hurrying to catch a plane. But plans are made to be changed, and instead Sherry sat down for the talk that led to Bob's "surrender"—the watershed of his life. Ever since, his conversation has been sprinkled with references to "before" and "after."

Bob walked on a cloud for weeks. It was like a honeymoon, the first rapturous days of a new relationship. He even caught himself singing out loud one day walking through gloomy, cavernous Pennsylvania Station. "Why am I singing?" he wondered, "I haven't sung in years."

He told the Tuesday group about that, and later in the same meeting he asked, "How do you talk to a Jewish person?" The story came out. He had called a friend, and his wife had answered.

"You sound tired, Cynthia."

"And why not? My mother, who's always been hard to live with, is dying of cancer and I've been spending every afternoon with her at the hospital. I'm exhausted."

"Have you been going to your house of worship?" asked Bob.

"No, why?"

"Well, when you pour water out of a pitcher, as you've been doing every day, you have to go somewhere to fill it up again."

"We've known you for years, Bob. We know you're not religious. So what you say makes good sense."

When Bob told Sherry Day the story, Sherry chuckled, "Of course you're not religious; you're *alive!*"

Months later Bob had his chance to witness to this couple and let them know where his words had come from.

Another Tuesday Bob was beaming. He had talked the day before to a taxi driver. Late for an appointment with an art director, he hailed a cab. The driver started the conversation by saying, "I'm glad you're going downtown because I've got to borrow some money and then I'm going to the race track. I know it's wrong. I haven't been there for a year. When I drive someone out there I put on blinders so I can't see it. I'm crazy to gamble. I have a wife and two kids. I need help!"

"You're like an alcoholic, aren't you?" suggested Bob.

"Yeah."

By now they had pulled up to the curb. Bob said, "We all go through some kind of a hell." He told him about his own, and about his commitment and the fellowship group, and then asked him about his faith.

"I'm Jewish."

"Well, we all pray to the same God. May I pray for you?"

"Sure."

"Right now, here?"

"Yes, I think I'd like that."

He put his hand on the driver's arm and asked God to be with his new friend. As he opened his eyes, the driver smiled. "Gee, I feel better already."

* * *

Another person Bob Arnold helped was a member of the Tuesday group. When John came to town he was referred to Faith at Work by a Christian girl he had dated at the University of Colorado who was "different." He soon discovered that Bob, too, had what made the difference.

One night he showed up at Bob's apartment. Over the noise of the whining hoists of the newspaper plant across the way he and Bob talked for an hour or two. As he was leaving John said, "I believe, but . . ."

"What is this *but?*" Bob asked.

"The Lord hasn't spoken to me."

"Look here. I don't know much about this, but I don't think God is going to come right out and speak to you audibly. Let's pray."

Later, as John started down the steps, in his excitement he walked past the elevator. Bob called him back.

John laughed. "Isn't it wonderful? It's fantastic! All I needed was fellowship."

18 /
Faith at Work
in the Pocono Mountains

*W*e had always had "house parties" or conferences at Calvary
House from the earliest days of Sam Shoemaker's ministry—
smallish ones were meetings for the "metropolitan team" in the
old group days, weekends for *Evangel* friends and readers, or for
students and/or the clergy. The largest gathering came at the end
of May, when Gramercy Park itself, with its willows and maples in
leaf and the flowering borders in bloom, looked like an oasis in the
dusty Manhattan scene. But when Sam Shoemaker had moved to
Pittsburgh and his successors showed less and less enthusiasm for
ecumenical gatherings, this May weekend was abandoned and our
whole conference program slipped badly. I, for one, while more
enthusiastic than ever about apartment meetings and monthly,
church-centered evenings for lay-witness evangelism, hesitated to
initiate in new locations conferences as ambitious as the old
weekends had been. For one thing our office work had multiplied
alarmingly and, both at "61" and after Faith at Work, Inc., had
established itself at 8 West 40th Street, we all seemed hard put to
keep our heads above water with the growing magazine work
alone.

However, "man proposes, God disposes." A New York team met
faithfully once a week and voices were regularly raised in favor of
reviving an adequate plan for the kind of conference which would
make it possible for magazine readers, friends, and enquirers to

"come apart" and find refreshment and new direction under the personal leadership of the Sherry Days and the Arthur Whites of the wider fellowship.

One Thursday night in February 1953, two brave souls* actually offered to tour the countryside to look for an adequate facility where we might revive the spring conference that following May. At the very next meeting their report sounded like "aces all aces": a complex of hotels known as "Pocono Crest" would provide for us at impressively low rates. Their acres of woodland and forest were a mere ninety miles west of New York City and, besides a grassy campus, a small lake, tennis courts, and riding horses were featured in the brochures which our teammates handed us that night.

As I sat there moderating the team my secret doubts choked in my throat and I heard myself saying, "O.K. Let's go." And with that we quickly chose a number of committees to think through the program, issue invitations, and arrange for books. As usual, Bertha Elliott acted as a coördinating genius, and the magazine itself heralded forth the good news in the most cordial terms in two successive full-page announcements.

The sixteen who stepped to the front in that, to us, memorable first year included a variety of personnel which, it seems clear, only God Himself could have provided. Here, at the extremes in the age differential, were Sherry Day, "Sam Shoemaker's oldest friend" (so-called) and Hugh Magee, a senior at Yale. Dolf Unger, not long out of an Indonesian prison camp, proposed an ecumenical communion service as part of the Sunday worship, while two Bible students, several men and women experienced in leading small groups, and at least one notable platform speaker had their special contributions.

When we finally arrived at Pocono Crest and found a quiet spot for our first team meeting, most of us felt like babes in the woods, a bit lost as to our major responsibility, until Sherry, as might have been expected, clarified our thoughts in three or four brief minutes by cheerily announcing, "Well, one thing is clear. Each of us has found forgiveness and a brand new way of life. Whoever comes just let's tell 'em that."

From that point on it was fun. Even the stipulation that, in order

---

* John Beck, assistant editor of *The Evangel*, and Dorothy Bennett, whose charming children's stories had already been translated and re-published in China.

to qualify for the special hotel rates, we must produce 150 conferees seemed unimportant, and sure enough in they came on the Friday afternoon and evening—along with torrents of rain—226 all told. Rooms were clean and ready. Tea and a short preview of the weekend were provided for the early arrivals. And when we met above the dining hall that first night, with Gardner Tewksbury at the piano, the room overflowed with as typical a cross section of Americans as one could hope to see.

Actually, it rained every single day that first conference—a phenomenon not to be repeated—but no one seemed to care. One young married woman, a nurse, who had come mainly to please her mother-in-law, found something she had been looking for all her life in the small groups, and quite spontaneously decided to try living under God's direction as an experiment. Her riding boots were of no use, but something happened to her which, in the last meeting, she described in such a real but slightly unintelligible way that she had the whole crowd laughing their encouragement. "Anyway," she finished, with an emphatic toss of her head, "it works!" And that, over the eleven years of the Pocono conferences, summed up the discovery of many.

For people concerned about the nation and the evil influences so widely at work, it was encouraging to see the numbers grow. The third or fourth year, with a greatly enlarged team, we registered about 600, using buildings that Pocono Crest had ordinarily never before opened until midsummer. But, with the advice of the management, and for various reasons relating to the quality of the conferences, we then set a top limit of 550 and a waiting list. Through the magazine we urged friends to be guided and not to drift into another conference just to be among old friends, but rather to consider making their places available to newcomers, if possible sending a friend from a home church or neighborhood who had never had the chance to experience such an event.

At the same time the stronger teams were led to pack a variety of important Christian principles into the conference programs. Often on the first evening it became our practice to choose knowledgeable speakers to outline the special world problems pressing for Christian solutions so that, in turn, the more personal questions of individuals' sins and possibilities might be considered with some definite relation to the world in which we live.

Early in each conference, team speakers in platform meetings then moved on to that neglected subject called *sin*. Sherry Day had long since established as a basic principle in discovering vital faith "fearless dealing with sin" and had helpfully redefined sin as "anything standing as a barrier between the individual and God or between a Christian and another person," all of which was briefly but clearly reviewed. That gave the team large latitude, and while we were aware that many seekers found God through "affirmation" and encouragement, many others came to the point of deciding to yield themselves to Him by seeing what a mess they had made of things and how desperately they needed forgiveness and a new chance.

There were always several early morning group "quiet times," all on a voluntary basis, for those who wanted to start the day with leaders who could suggest ways to use the Bible in daily, personal devotions. Simultaneously each morning an unhurried, large team meeting for all leaders was also held before breakfast in an upper room apart from the general conference.

One of the secrets of the success of these weekends was undoubtedly the opportunity they gave both for personal quiet and meditation and also for leisurely talks between two people, one of whom had found a measure of new life and the other a person who needed it and perhaps was looking for it.

One year, noticing that more than a few people happened by the conference grounds a bit late, perhaps somewhat skeptical and with no clear intention of participating seriously in the proceedings, we set up a special talk-it-over group on the lawn to welcome such strays and any others present who had failed to be assigned to a regular group.

The story of Rhett, a senior executive in a Pennsylvania steel company, is perhaps the best kind of a summary of such an operation and should also answer several questions about the results, as well as the aims, of the Pocono Conference itself.

Ralston Young and I had been fielding questions and encouraging comments on the early morning Bible study in such a group for half an hour or so when Rhett and his equally sophisticated companion approached the meeting. Theoretically we were supposed to be ready to receive just such latecomers; but there was something in the air of the self-assurance these men emanated which put my back up and quite reversed the outgoing attitude with which I had started the group. We made room for them and, as they moved their folding chairs across the grass and into the circle, I found myself pleading with the Almighty to make me loving and hospitable. He did. Again smiles prevailed all around and the discussion continued, but since our business friends had not the ghost of an idea of what the Bible study had been—or even of what a meeting of this kind was all about—their remarks seemed strangely irrelevant and their questions remained almost completely unanswered.

As we broke up for luncheon I stepped over to the stockier of the two and shaking his hand said, "I'm sorry. You really didn't get much of a hearing."

"Thanks. That's all right," he replied genially. "I'm afraid we were butting in. We should have come earlier."

"No," I went on, "this meeting was arranged for fellows just like you. I don't know whether I have any adequate answers to the points you raised, and I do have a luncheon meeting, but if you would like to talk some more, I'd be free to join you here about two o'clock. By any chance would you like to meet again?"

"Sure would," replied the other, and so it was arranged.

Soon after luncheon the two of us pulled a couple of wicker chairs under an apple tree on one side of the lawn. People were walking to and fro, but any fear that I may have had about my adequacy to deal with the queries of a successful businessman soon evaporated, for my companion began talking at once—not asking questions but simply relating the story of his life. He obviously wanted to talk, and I had learned to listen.

It seemed that as a young high-school fellow he had landed an excellent job in a steel mill down in Alabama or Georgia, but he had to lie about his age in order to get accepted. He described several of his early occupations and spoke of his promotions. It was clear that he had often moved up the ladder at the expense of someone else and occasionally by reverting to the dishonesty with which he had begun his career. He must have gone on for almost an hour, content with merely a nod or a grunt from me, when he suddenly leaned back, looked me straight in the face, and to my complete surprise exclaimed, "Now what on earth could God Almighty do with a fellow like that?"

Without thinking, I stared back and answered "Plenty."

He laughed. "No, you're too optimistic. You see, in the past I've attended evangelistic meetings and even got pretty well steamed up. In fact I've made a Christian decision or two in my day, but they never lasted."

"Look, old man," I said, "this business of following Christ is not a matter of simply making a decision. It means starting to live in a wholly new way. It's an unencumbered life, often requiring a willingness to break for a time at least with the old crowd—perhaps even change your job. It's a bit like getting aboard a ship. You have to repack your belongings and leave a heap of things behind on shore. You may find the life aboard the ship a great experience or you may dislike it. You may know where the ship is heading or you may not be very clear about the destination. But you realize that the pilot of the Christian ship is Jesus Christ Himself. You live under His orders, and for many a day. Furthermore, you don't go running around jeopardizing the lives of other passengers by the things you do. To begin with, you may have to learn to live on a brand new schedule and make friends with people you've never known before."

Since this interested him, I went on and briefly told of some of the turning points in my own life which had challenged me to change well-laid plans, hand over small but cherished assets, and drastically reschedule my time. And I gave him chapter and verse of some of the amazing results flowing from acts of faith and trust. "It's a great life," I assured him. "You'll be surprised."

Then once again, to my own surprise, he looked fixedly at me and firmly said, "I'll buy that." His absolute sincerity almost bowled me over.

Then, "If you feel that way, we'd better pray about it," I suggested. "You're not promising anything to me or to anyone else except the Almighty. But you may have things to say to God. I'll just listen in."

Unlike many a person who is asked to pray aloud, Rhett didn't hesitate a moment. Despite the strollers, despite distant noises from the kitchen and the hotel rooms, he merely leaned forward, clasped his head in his hands, and told God quite directly how sorry he was for his dishonesties, his self-indulgence, and the ruthlessness in his business life. Then I said a short prayer, and we stood up.

Something had happened. There was no doubt about that. One could see it in his face and feel it in his handshake. A mystery? Yes, but how tangible the results!

Fortunately I felt restrained from offering one single word of advice. We broke up the talk and I walked briskly back to my own room. But my new friend apparently couldn't keep silent. He had to say hello to those who passed by. He had to stop and reply to one or two. In essence, he made it apparent to several of these that he had unexpectedly found a whole new release from pressure and from his old life. That night at a crowded gathering of the whole conference, at an appropriate point he felt compelled to raise his hand and, to the astonishment of many, he spoke of the power and mercy of God as if he had been experiencing such blessings for years. Friends from his home town rejoiced with him and more than one looked me up later to ask, "What in the world did you do to Rhett?"

"Nothing at all," I replied truthfully, "nothing but listen and suggest that he make things right with God."

At the same time his wife, vindicated in her expectations, claimed that she had a new husband, and soon afterwards we heard of spiritual influences emanating from their home.

Of course further business advancement now opened like an Aladdin's cave and according to last reports he is today heading one of the steel company's most important divisions. But that, in a real way, is unimportant. On a 1973 Christmas card he wrote a longhand note about a special avenue of service he had found in the probation and "big brother" work in his city. I must say that his card transmitted a flavor of joy which seemed especially appropriate on a folder with Christmas greetings.

* * *

It is quite natural for people who have never been to such conferences to ask, "Does it last?" Rhett's story is a relevant answer to that. Others too hastily conclude that a new sect or movement has begun and wonder how "the Poconos" relate to The First Presbyterian Church on Main Street, U.S.A. A friend who read this chapter while it was still in manuscript form asked me if she could send me an account of what happened to a group of friends from Worcester, Massachusetts, who found themselves at the Poconos after they had been turned down by the registration team of an earlier conference.

Dorothy Howard writes: "Ten of us in Worcester had found God in a real way two or three years before we had thought of going to a religious conference. We felt a need for growth and fellowship and had written Eugenia Price, the author, for help. Genie had not only responded promptly and suggested our trying a Faith at Work conference, but she had anticipated what might happen and told us that, should the Statler-Hilton conference in New York be closed out for want of space, we should register for one in the Poconos in the spring.

"This we did, but as the time drew near for us to leave for the Poconos, we began to wonder what it would be like. Coming from a liberal church background, none in the group had ever attended such a conference, and we were not sure what we might be getting into. Upon arrival, of course, we registered and then found our way to the first meeting late in the afternoon. Here we were first of all impressed with the friendliness of the many people already present and immediately felt a part. This helped to banish our fears.

"The opening night we walked under the stars across the lawn to a huge building. Flags of all nations hung from the ceiling, and on the platform we saw a group of men of various ages. When the singing of hymns like "Faith of Our Fathers" was concluded, a young fellow who turned out to be Bruce Larson, the coordinator of the conference, stepped to the microphone and got his straightforward message across with a sense of humor which immediately made us glad that we had come. From the very start that night, we realized that this was not a sanctimonious gathering but what we called a fellowship.

"Then came a woman who spoke of the joy she had found at simply being freed to be herself. She declared that she had been a pretender, ever trying to make people think that she was a super person merely because she was a nominal Christian. In reality she had discovered that she was on a journey and that she had not by any means arrived at the full Christian way of life. She went on to refer to both her failures and her victories. I must admit that at first we were embarrassed at this open, personal way of talking. However, three others who, in a similar way, were honest about themselves during the course of the evening, turned our embarrassment into amazement as we began to relate our own needs to theirs and discover a common ground for relationship in fellowship together.

"When we were assigned to small groups we felt a bit nervous at being separated and put into groups with strangers, but it didn't take long for the ice to break as the leader of each group of ten invited us to introduce ourselves but only to speak about our needs if we felt so led. I do not know what happened in the other groups, but I, for one, was not about to say anything! This struck me as a bit too much, so, since there was no feeling of being forced, I passed.

"The conference lasted for a full weekend and we attended every meeting. After talking over the events and witnesses among ourselves, some of us decided to take the plunge and talk, but it wasn't until the last small group meeting that any of us had the courage to do this. Then, however, came a release and joy and a sense of freedom we simply had not had before.

"The important point for us in the long run was that we left the conference grounds with a feeling that we had glimpsed a bit of what the fellowship of Christians was all about. It had been a cleansing, joyous, caring experience, and we returned to Worcester with the resolution to try out what we had learned in our own church when the time was ripe. Only a year later we had our own first Faith at Work conference with about 120 people attending, and a goodly number of neighbors made their first true commitment to the Lord Jesus as they listened to personal talks like the ones which had moved us. Real life here without having to drive a mile!"

*   *   *

One of the most memorable aspects of the Pocono conferences was the number of Bermudians who joined in as the conferences proceeded year by year. Howard Dickinson, a medical man, Brigadier Charles Watt of the Salvation Army in Bermuda, and Commander Geoffrey Kitson each had a special part in encouraging their friends and neighbors to combine a refreshing vacation with a spiritual opportunity by a day's journey by plane and bus to Pocono Crest. And how many stories could be told of miracles which happened among this group of visitors alone! Of them all the one about Herbert Knight, entitled "A Nickel Does It" will more than suffice.

By age thirty, Herbie had come to hate most everyone. He hated white men, he hated blacks, of which he was one, most of all he hated himself. When *delirium tremens* became par for the course, most of the doctors in the mental institution which became his

home declared his case to be hopeless. However, "Doctor Howard," though he had had no professional connection with Herbie,
now and again would call in to see him in his room. Herbie, Howard admitted, had pretty serious problems, but he would never say
he was hopeless. To Howard, as to members of Alcoholics
Anonymous, the last word had to be God's.

One spring day, a few weeks before a Pocono Conference, Dr.
Dickinson adopted a new approach. "Herbie," he said, "just now,
when the dogwoods are in bloom in Pennsylvania, a few of my
friends and I visit one of the loveliest spots in the world, the
Pocono Mountains. We want you to go with us. You'll be our
guest."

Herbie merely rolled over on his bed to face the wall. But the
doctor returned the next day and the next always saying, "You'd
better come. I can promise you it will be a lot different from St.
Brendan's Hospital."

It was not until almost the last possible moment that a miracle
took place. Herbie was still in a sullen mood, but he surprised
even himself and agreed to go. For one thing, he had begun to
think of all the alcohol there might be waiting for him along the
way. It was also a case of *anything to get out of here!*

Thirty or forty Bermudians, most of them happy ones, journeyed
that year to the American mountain retreat. On the plane Herbie
saw the first chance to satisfy his private hopes, with a shot of
Scotch just a few feet away. But with "No, thanks just the same,"
the doctor dismissed the hostess and Herbie slumped further
down in his chair. The bus that carried the party on their second
lap passed through increasingly beautiful country, but all Herbie
saw were the roadside taverns. He made a mental note of the one
on the very edge of the conference grounds. At the hotel he found
that he disliked everyone he met. He sat at the back of a few
meetings, but for the most part he simply sulked in the room he
and Howard Dickinson occupied together.

On the last morning of the conference, after a restless night,
Herbie rose early, not for Bible study and prayer, but thinking
about that nearby tavern. At such an hour, however, he found
nothing open, so he turned toward the lake he had noticed shining
through the trees. Trudging slowly along the road, he came to the
edge of the water and scuffled on in the sand. He was completely
disconsolate, longing for the drink that was poison to him; but

perhaps a few new thoughts were struggling in his mind. Suddenly, as he kicked at the sand, his toe struck a small bright disc and tossed it up on the beach ahead. It was nothing more valuable than an American five-cent piece, a nickel, but as Herbie rubbed it clean, something caught his eye—not the date or the design of the coin, but four short words, put there by a Christian legislature years before: *In God We Trust.*

Herbie's memory is not quite clear about what happened next. All he can state for sure is that suddenly he found himself on his knees in the sand, crying out to God for help. With a deep sense of need, the shame of his wasted life overcame him. He says he felt a sorrow he had never known before. "Take the drink Lord. I can't make it, but You can," he cried. And as he knelt there, forgiveness and peace settled like a mantle on his soul.

Brushing himself off, but holding on to that small bright coin, he hurried back to the dining hall. Breakfast had just commenced, and some of the very men whom he had detested drew him to a table. Within himself he felt a new and loving friendliness, and a revived hunger for food *and* for life. Of all the bacon and eggs he ever tasted, these, he says, seemed by all odds the best.

He was still in time, too, for the last conference meeting. He found this to be a chance for individuals to give a personal summing up, with all sorts of people disclosing their discoveries of the last few days. His host, the doctor, was on the platform, and surprisingly enough, Herbie felt eager to speak. With five or six others he raised his hand, but only to hear the announcement of a hymn. That nettled him. Perhaps Dr. Dickinson didn't feel he deserved a turn! He slipped out and walked upstairs as far as his room, but God did not let him go. *How foolish,* he thought, *to miss this chance after all I have just been given.* Back in the meeting he tried again, and this time Howard noticed him and joyfully called him to come forward.

People say it was hard to tell who was happier, the doctor or the patient, as Herbie walked down the aisle. Then he turned, faced the crowd, and told briefly just what had happened. An audible murmur of praise rose from those who filled the room.

You should see Herbert Knight now! On his return to Bermuda many of his buddies met him with derision. "Come off it and have a drink." "No thanks," answered Herbie, frequently trying to describe to such friends what God through Christ had done for him in the Poconos, but his change mystified some and maddened others. In a short time he left the building trade and took a job on the staff of a small hotel, the Willowbank, which is run by a fellowship of Christians. As his talents developed, so his occupations multiplied. At one point he might be carrying bags, at another running a movie projector, but always it was the people who owned the luggage and viewed the pictures who became his friends, and especially their children. Today, of the four or five top staff who are operating the enlarged guest house, Herbie is definitely one.

* * *

Soon after Bruce Larson came on the staff there began to be "Poconos" all over the country—small weekends in local churches, big hotel meetings in Tennessee and Wisconsin—while large conference teams took on gatherings quite similar to the Poconos. Bruce's magic touch, under God, "reproduced reproducers," and one team picture I have before me shows sixty-four men and women on a New York City Conference team who look quite capable of changing the face of America if not of the world!

During these same years, however, the Pocono Conferences themselves were handed over to a strong local team in Bethlehem, Pennsylvania, and to this a few of us on the FAW board made a vigorous protest. Not that we were anything but positive about Bethlehem, but we felt that our younger colleagues failed to appreciate the great benefit derived by gathering together, at least once a year, the top spiritual leadership we were in touch with. Increasingly, the Poconos had demonstrated what a Faith at Work conference could be, and our participants could and did carry away with them patterns to follow as they might wish in their own respective work. We were also learning from each other what God-given new things worked to help people find God, and what insights God was giving to those on various spiritual firing lines. Claxton Monro, rector of St. Stephen's Church, Houston, Texas, for instance, struck a resounding note one May in telling how his parish had incorporated lay-witnessing into their church services. His message on prophecy, too, gave us a whole new dimension to evangelism.

Such leadership also corrected our thinking in a double way, by helping us first to review the direction in which we individually were traveling, and at the same time to check again on the quality of our own personal lives. Somehow, isolated leadership meetings tend to develop points of view; but at the Poconos, as in Keswick, England, before us, leaders seeking deeper faith were brought into a blood brotherhood. Each of us needs to see these basic patterns whether we accept them lock, stock, and barrel or not. The Poconos gave these to us in a strikingly cumulative way.

19 /

Bermuda —
Bridge between Two Worlds

A little over seven hundred miles southeast of New York City, and even closer to Cape Hatteras, rises the green-colored, rocky crescent of Bermuda, that speck in the North Atlantic which marks the top of an ancient volcanic ridge. Once a British Crown Colony and still an integral part of the Commonwealth, Bermuda strikes some visitors as more British than Britain itself! Yet tourism, its chief current industry, looks to North America. The true "Bermuda Triangle" usually has both London and New York at its vertices.

Life on this lovely twenty-five-mile-long chain of rocky islands is a product of two worlds and, in this jet age, a bridge between the Old World and the New. For the airplane now spans the oceans as effectively as Roman roads connected the nations of the Mediterranean centuries ago. Thus Bermuda speaks with many accents, some pious, some pagan. In shops, guesthouses, and even on TV, one hears constant references to the Bible, still the world's best-seller—ancient passages where one finds the eternal truths on which the Founding Fathers built America. Countless ecumenical groups meet weekly in every section of the island. On Sundays Norman Vincent Peale, as well as visiting evangelists and local pastors, use most of the air time on one main Bermuda broadcasting station.

*　　*　　*

It has been said of Americans generally that, when it comes to speaking of their personal faith, even the Christians among them are tongue-tied. Faith itself is prevalent, but clear, comprehensive expressions of Bible truths are not characteristic of daily converse in the United States. Countless Bermudians on every level of the social scale can give a lead. Here is a tale which points up the possibilities.

Howard Dickinson, one of a family long-established on the island and today a senior medical man on the staff of St. Brendan's Hospital in Bermuda, began his pre-med work at St. John's College, Oxford. It was there he first listened with an open mind to a fellow student's account of the elementary facts of the story of Jesus Christ; and as this other man talked in a simple, compelling way Howard accepted what he heard as a trial basis for his own life. When he returned to Bermuda he was not only qualified to practice medicine but ready to bring faith to his friends at home.

Among these was a young commission merchant, Harold, who was fairly screaming for help. Not merely did Harold need faith to temper the materialism of his occupation; he needed an answer to alcoholism which was fast ruining his life and his business. Dr. Howard and a Philadelphia visitor whose husband was also an alcoholic went to work. They offered Harold the same power the doctor had found in England, and through them he found a fresh experience of God. He stopped drinking and began to say his prayers. Buttressed by pots of black coffee, he and his gallant wife began meeting regularly each week at the home of the doctor and his wife.

About the same time an American couple, one of whose lives had been fouled up by alcoholism, arrived on the island with news of a new group known as "Alcoholics Anonymous." They provided Harold with twelve specific steps which they vowed had brought them personal faith and freedom. And almost overnight an A.A. outpost appeared and weekly meetings commenced further out on the island.

Meanwhile the Dickinsons' group, made up of friends and patients (and incidentally the first house group on the island), continued to flourish. Then a once-a-week, ecumenical breakfast meeting composed entirely of men took over the kitchen of a church in Hamilton. Within a few years some fifteen different groups were functioning on this same weekly basis.

The secret of Howard's own steadiness lay in the habit of "keeping a quiet time with God," a practice he had discovered and started in England. To any inquirers he put it this way: "There is only one absolute requirement for continuing in the Christian life: a constantly renewed relationship with God. In order that this may happen the average man or woman should observe what has become widely known as the "quiet time," that is, a very special time set aside regularly, daily, when one can be undisturbed and wait unhurriedly upon God. . . . Beginners sometimes ask how much time such meditation requires. A famous leader once answered this question by saying that we should spend at least as much time in preparing the immortal soul for the day as we do in dressing the mortal body. My own aim is for an hour each morning, but for various reasons this is often not realized. You may find at first that a much shorter period is all you can digest. In any case it is obviously not the duration of time that counts but the quality of the content."

Dr. Dickinson further maintained: "The struggle to establish regularity in this God-given habit gets easier as we go on, but there is always a pull in the opposite direction. A fresh morning newspaper has for me, as I expect for most men, an almost irresistible attraction; and as a rather cowardly way around this distraction, I've arranged that my paper should come by mail later in the day!"

Before long, allies appeared in various places and several, adopting Dr. Howard's lead, established midweek groups in their own homes or churches. The owner of a chain of supermarkets hopefully chose Wednesday noon as a spiritually productive time and asked a few other business friends to share a simple luncheon in his office. An ex-Navy flier who, in a time of extreme danger, had dedicated his life to a special outreach among young people, found that he was able to make his Bermuda home a full-time center for Christian youth work.

Another of the most active believers on the Island eventually came out of the British Navy. Geoffrey Kitson, having married a Bermudian, settled there after World War II. He soon became extremely successful in organizing travel and other business enterprises, some of which brought him to the United States. On a stopover in New York City, while flipping through the amusement pages of the *New York Times*, looking for a new movie or a show, he came upon a large notice with Billy Graham's handsome face dominating the space.

"By Jove, what a lark it would be," he thought. "I'll run across to Madison Square Garden and see what this fellow is up to!"

The doorman of the hotel encouraged him to go and have a look. "But you'll do well to get over to the Garden right away," he advised. "Crowds from all over. You'll just about make it."

Geoff Kitson took this advice with a grain of salt, but as he approached the great auditorium he was surprised to see the lines and lines of people, young and old, converging from every side. As he entered, he discovered he was only in time to claim a seat in the very top balcony. As he gazed down from his eerie perch, he heard an organ playing. After a bit, a beautifully robed, well-disciplined choir rose and emitted such a rich volume of melodious hymn-singing that the visitor's Scottish, musically appreciative soul fairly vibrated, and he realized that he was already getting his money's worth.

When Billy Graham at last arose and, Bible in hand, stepped to the loud-speaker, Geoffrey Kitson's mood had altered radically. All at once it seemed as if Graham was speaking loudly, clearly, and *directly to him*. It was as if he had become the evangelist's only listener. Briskly, point by point, Billy underlined a few of the basic ingredients of Christian faith, and against a kind of mirror of perfection, Kitson saw lighted up his own shabbiness and self-indulgence.

The evangelist closed with his usual suggestion that those who had things to settle with God should come forward for a prayer of dedication. Kitson felt himself impelled, almost driven, by a force far outweighing his natural reluctance. He began to descend, balcony by balcony, and then pushed down the main, center aisle with troops of others beside and in front and behind him, until he stood wedged in and silent directly in front of the speaker. As the evangelist interceded for the hundreds of individuals who by their very presence in the center aisle had already made an act of submission to Almighty God, the hush was broken only by Billy's moving prayer which somehow included everyone who heard it and expressed the new intention of each.

As for Geoff Kitson, something happened; he felt both poignantly beloved by God and freshly cleansed and forgiven. He glimpsed something of what he might have been, and with God's power might still become. His family, his business, his daily life swept into remembrance, but it was Billy's assurance of the good which God was then and there doing within him that most gripped him.

Back at his hotel as he sprawled on the bed, not bothering at first to undress, the realization grew that this evening he had turned a corner and stepped onto a brighter, better road.

Two days later as he flew out of New York, Madison Square Garden seemed a long distance away, but the revolution of the mass meeting had not been in vain, and a second chapter was not far off. Within a week after reaching Bermuda he unexpectedly ran smack into Howard Dickinson on a street corner and was soon pouring out his whole New York story.

Howard smiled, "Don't you know what happened to you in New York?" Geoff shook his head. "You were converted." With alarm Geoff ejaculated, "My God, not *that!*" But then was quick to accept the doctor's diagnosis and the suggestion that he sit in with the small study group at the Dickinsons' home the following Tuesday. At succeeding meetings, week by week, he met others who were finding some of the same new freedom that he was experiencing. He discovered that the parts of the Bible on which the Tuesday group was focused were as fresh as contemporary life itself. Furthermore he decided to start the practice of daily private prayer at home. Before long he even looked up the vicar of his church, stopping by the latter's study one day, on the way home from work, and somewhat hesitantly offering his services. The vicar himself opened the door and, as he laughingly admitted later, almost had a nervous breakdown when he saw Geoff and heard he had come to offer his services in some capacity as a layman. "For two years I've been praying for a man like you to help me," he declared, "and now that you're here I can hardly believe it. In a couple of weeks I'll have you teaching my own adult Bible class!" Geoff thought this was not quite the job for a new convert, but armed with a concordance and a Phillip's translation of the New Testament—and with the encouragement of the doctor's group—things caught on in a big way. After this, Geoff got a few of his business staff together and told them the whole story with the result that something very much like the doctor's Bible group sprang up in the form of a voluntary meeting, a half-hour before business hours, one morning a week in the office. Geoffrey Kitson also became the prime mover and chief money-raiser in a program to construct his church's first parish hall and Christian education building.

*   *   *

Dr. Dickinson had an elderly patient, a Mrs. Zuill, who kept pestering him about a little magazine she subscribed to. Each issue, she said, gave her a boost and she always kept a copy on her bedside table. The doctor had far more reading matter than he knew what to do with, and the appearance and name of the periodical recommended by his patient he thought rather pious (at that time it was called *The Evangel*). However, after much procrastination he at last felt bound to carry off a copy of the journal. To his utter amazement, on opening it up, he came straight on a story similar to, and every bit as exciting as, the New York episode of his friend Geoff. He found equally surprising pages as he read further: a pertinent editorial on the possibility of applying one's faith to business and professional life, a sermon reporting several examples of spiritual healing, and a vast number of names and addresses of people active in fellowship and group meetings in innumerable parts of the world, even in quite obscure places in lands overseas. He was further intrigued by the magazine's masthead. While it was obviously an Anglican or Episcopal publication, it had a Presbyterian as its editor, not to mention a board of men and women with a variety of denominational backgrounds. The table of contents "rang all his bells" and prior to taking out a subscription for himself he became his patient's most insistent borrower.

In one issue *The Evangel* reported a rather spectacular piece of news from England. An adventurous band of Anglican clergy and laymen had taken over a beautifully located inn, "Lee Abbey," in the Lorna Doone country of North Devonshire to use as a retreat center for evangelistic conferences and person-to-person encounters between inquiring visitors and a carefully chosen staff. Originators of the program were men known as Christians with a vital and contagious quality of life. The New York magazine ran a prominent announcement about the purchase of Lee Abbey and described how a small bequest left to one member of the board, which he immediately gave over to a common fund, had clinched the acquisition of the property and put the scheme into operation. The New York magazine later printed a descriptive article with pictures of the property and of the dedicatory services.

Howard Dickinson was impressed. Later on, he flew to England and after a week at Lee Abbey began to think about the possibility of a similar venture in Bermuda, and to long that it might happen. He already knew the work of Dr. Abraham Vereide in the U.S.A. and had visited Fellowship House in Washington. There a few individuals, living sacrificially, were capturing people's imagination for Christ. A breakfast group like the original one in Seattle on the West Coast had sprung up in the Senate, and soon there was one in the House, both under the auspices of International Christian Leadership (now the Fellowship Foundation, Inc.).

When the first of several of Dr. Vereide's I.C.L. conferences was held at the Princess Hotel in Hamilton, Bermuda, Howard Dickinson was there. So were several of his business and professional friends. Together they jointly sponsored the event with a team from Washington. Anticipation ran high.

Most everyone knows the usual objectives of a Bermuda vacation. But there were a few Bermudians at that conference from various groups on the island with whom Howard had discussed the Lee Abbey idea and a plan to give vacationers something more than a conventional holiday. The first evening Canon Wallace Bird of London made an inspiring talk in which he pointed out the strategic location of Bermuda for those with spiritual vision of the world-wide nature of God's work. Then Norman Grubb spoke, underlining the Bible truth that things God wants to bring to pass *are already in being.* Norman went on to point out that to bring some specific thing to reality in human experience it takes but a single man who has the vision and in whose heart God can put the conviction, *Yes, I believe it.* That night, at the moment he heard this, Howard Dickinson felt led to say quietly, "Yes, I believe it."

The next morning Dr. Howard announced to the conference that, on waking, he felt that God had told him to take a first step in carrying out the plans which several in the Bermuda groups had in mind by opening a special bank account. Immediately, there was a general sense that this was indeed of God.

Soon after, Norman Grubb and "Abram" Vereide drove with him to both the Inverurie and the Belmont to see if either of these hotels might be the place God would be making available for work like that at Lee Abbey. The real estate market was volatile, but it took considerably more time to discover such a spot.

* * *

The first visit to "Willowbank" came in 1960 following a breakfast group meeting. Howard Dickinson says he can never forget the date as it was the anniversary of his own spiritual birthday, his turning-point at Oxford, a good many years before. There were five of the inner team in his car. They passed the entrance once but, since the property had recently been vacated, they drove back to have a look at the interior of the main building with its beautiful cedar beams. Then standing outside, gazing westward across the open sea toward Hatteras, all unanimously agreed that this was unquestionably what they had been looking for.

In the beginning the Willowbank Community consisted of little more than a devoted cook, a housekeeper, and two or three guests. Dr. Vereide came to visit it, and when it was finally dedicated that November, he recommended Roy and Evelyne Cook as a couple especially qualified to head up such a Christian community. They were working over three thousand miles away in Salem, Oregon; but despite the rather short notice they, too, caught a vision of the opportunity looming up in Bermuda. After further thought and prayer, since they were free to do so, they decided almost overnight to proceed to the Island to spearhead whatever might develop.

From its inception Willowbank glistened with innumerable blessings. From time to time plenty of problems also arose. But over the years many, many people have found a living faith there. Countless others have received new inspiration for living or the re-charging of spiritual batteries which had run dry. At the end of fifteen years the accommodations had been increased to provide for over a hundred guests and cleared of all indebtedness; a victory celebration took place with special speakers such as Norman Grubb and Corrie ten Boom from overseas.

Early in 1977 the Willowbank Trustees announced the purchase of a second, beautiful sea-front property known as "Southlands." With the income from the surprising success of their Christian guesthouse there was a deep conviction that a series of nonprofit projects could and should be undertaken. These could not only contribute in special ways to the health and welfare of Bermudians but also to island visitors. The Willowbank board has always held that man's deepest need is spiritual and is convinced that, in fellowship, people will find a new dimension in their lives. For some this may mean discovering a vital, personal faith for the first time; for others it may mean the renewal of a faith which has become dull and meaningless.

With this kind of a background modern miracles are bound to continue. The beauty and resources of Southlands itself can have an effect on widely different kinds of people. Its magnificent shorefront and secluded woodland offer ideal assets for use in youth work. In one of its present buildings a project will probably be commenced to rehabilitate, month by month, a number of men and women who have been ill and hospitalized and need further care, and in some instances psychiatric help, before again taking up the responsibilities of normal living. Then there is the possibility of establishing centers for the treatment of those with serious problems such as drug addiction. As for Dr. Dickinson, he singles out alcoholism as the island's number one problem and hopes that Southlands will provide a very definite program to meet this challenge.

Two further likely developments at Southlands are a plan for the teaching and training of Christian leaders and the construction of a handsome Retirement Home such as does not yet exist on the island.

*   *   *

As a somewhat dramatic illustration of the reality of what many would call the true or spiritual "Bermuda Triangle"—and at the very time when this book was being polished for the printer—the news came that Cmdr. Geoffrey Kitson had accepted the presidency of Faith at Work, Inc. (U.S.A.). Geoff has lived in Bermuda since his retirement from the British Navy after World War II. Since F.A.W. today has its own premises, the Sam Shoemaker Building in Columbia, Maryland, he and his wife, Betty, at considerable personal sacrifice, will now be spending most of their time in the United States. Incidentally, Geoff is the first full-time layman to become the head of F.A.W., U.S.A.

When the previous president resigned to return to local parish work, the directors formed a "search committee" to choose a successor. Geoffrey Kitson became chairman. Then the qualifications of the next president were discussed and it soon became clear that, with new opportunities opening up ever more widely for F.A.W., the right man would be difficult to find—especially as he might already be happily engaged heading up some other important

Christian venture. Geoff says that one day the rather uncomfortable thought struck him that if no other suitable person emerged he should accept the presidency himself—on two conditions: (1) that his wife would also think this to be God's will and (2) that their older son who heads the family business would concur. A few weeks later the directors elected him unanimously with both conditions met.

One "gift of the Spirit" is hope, and because of this, true believers from the Apostle Paul on down over the centuries rejoice, even in a hostile and often very evil world. Occurrences such as the one described are themselves a cause of rejoicing. The change of leadership in this instance is in reality an *ex*change, and just as Willowbank once found its leadership in North America so now Bermuda's loss is America's gain.

*   *   *

Today we are all reminded by the press and TV, as well as by personal experience, that the *force* of evil, not the Source of good, is again gaining ascendency. The twentieth century, once heralded as a "bright and shining" age, has become a dangerous and confused one.

Those who focus on one side of the coin, see flagrant immorality, condoned by the false philosophy of permissiveness, and sophisticated weaponry in the hands of power-greedy men bent on destruction. Ruthlessness is displacing justice; apathy and stubbornness are more often than not taking the place of alertness and goodwill.

However, those who take the trouble to look at the other side of the coin find symbols of God's providence. Not a few then remember that the Creator's arm is "not foreshortened" and that He alone has the last word. They rejoice in His promises and experience renewed energy. They remember the courage and confidence of thousands of people like those whose stories are told in these pages.

What will the New Year of the twenty-first century reveal? If bells ring out in A.D. 2000, they will celebrate a victory of some kind. Instead of the old humanistic victories it could be a spiritual and perhaps a lasting one.

Index